Lisa Ann

Golf Training

In a refreshing departure from the "do-as-I-do" books by tour pros, LPGA Class A teaching pro Lisa Ann Hörst lays out a comprehensive, science-based program that will work for golfers of any age, sex, or ability level. *Golf Training* goes beyond the mechanics of the game and provides specific instruction and drills on a wide range of topics. You will learn:

- How to leverage the principles of golf training for rapid improvement.
- How to assess your strengths and weaknesses, and then set goals for breaking through to the next level of play.
- Effective drills to groove a great swing and correct swing errors.
- How to hit your long irons and fairway woods.
- The best practice strategy for dialing in your short irons and wedge play.
- The keys to effective chipping, pitching, putting, and bunker play.
- Mental training techniques for lowering pressure, releasing tension, controlling your emotions, boosting confidence, increasing motivation, and creating anchors for peak performance.
- The secrets of fitness conditioning, golf-specific strength training, and performance nutrition to elevate your quality of play and enjoyment.

Golf Training is not a book full of promises. It is a book for golfers who have made promises to themselves and are now ready to keep them. If you're just learning golf, this book is invaluable. If you're already a strong player, Lisa Ann challenges you to get even more from all levels of your game. This is the most comprehensive "guide to better golf" that I have seen.

—***Tom Ferrell,*** *author and journalist, founder of OnTour Media, Inc.*

Golf Training reveals that there is much more to being a great golfer than having a perfect swing. Lisa Ann Hörst covers all aspects of the game, including swing fundamentals, tips on how to practice, and mental and fitness training that will enable you to become the best player you can be. Anyone who really wants to improve their game can learn a lot from this book.

—***Karen Palacios-Jansen,*** *LPGA Teaching Professional,* Golf For Women *Top 50 Instructor, and developer of Cardiogolf™*

Golf Training will positively transform your golf game. Lisa Ann Hörst combines current scientific findings from kinesiology and sport psychology with years of experience as a golf pro to deliver a fresh approach to performance improvement. Here is a cohesive program for self-assessment and progressive change. I'm particularly taken with *Golf Training*'s brilliant coverage of sport psychology's best-kept secrets, including methods for improving motivation, confidence, visualization, fear management, anxiety control, concentration and focus, and performance rituals. It's all here in a beautifully written and illustrated book that will help you gain a competitive edge.

—Richard K. Fleming, Ph.D., assistant professor of psychology & researcher in behavior and performance at the University of Massachusetts Medical School

---

I like *Golf Training*! It is very well written, clear, and interesting, and it contains much new information. But the main thing that attracted me was the attention to the principles of learning that come from the scientific area of motor learning.

My experience with most other books on sport is that they are not written from a scientific perspective. Most such books are based either on best guesses about how to practice, how the author was taught, or how some famous professional player practices. The problem with such an approach is that many proven principles of practice are somewhat counterintuitive, and they are certainly different from what a commonsense understanding of practice would predict. Furthermore, many coaches and writers tend to resist these scientific principles, as they are apparently uncomfortable with these newer generalizations.

Golf Training pays strong attention to the scientifically based principles of practice. In fact, Lisa Ann Hörst devotes an entire chapter to the principles of practice as a kind of "bedrock," and then refers to these in the remaining chapters as justification for what she recommends for practice. I find these ideas to be current, the choice of principles carefully selected, and the applications to the game of golf appropriate. This is certainly a refreshing trend, and the book should be effective for one who is serious about learning the game.

—Richard Schmidt, Ph.D., president of Human Performance Research, author of Motor Learning and Performance, *and professor of psychology at the University of California, Los Angeles*

Golf Training

The Secrets to Effective Practice and a Lower Score (Finally!)

Lisa Ann Hörst
LPGA Class A Teaching Professional

Hörst Enterprises
Lancaster, Pennsylvania

Golf Training: The Secrets to Effective Practice and a Lower Score
First Edition, Spring 2004

Cover and inside photography copyright © 1997–2003 by Eric J. Hörst
Illustrations: Rob Hörst
Copy editor: Laura Jorstad
Project editor: Eric J. Hörst
Designer: Eric McCallister (www.McCallisterDesign.com)

Contact Information:
P.O. Box 8633
Lancaster, PA 17604
www.LisaAnnHorst.com

Library of Congress Cataloging-in-Publication Data
Hörst, Lisa Ann,
Golf Training: The Secrets to Effective Practice and a Lower Score / Lisa Ann Hörst—1st ed.
p. cm.
ISBN: 0-9744724-2-5
1. Sports—Golf. 2. Golf—Training.
I. Title.
Manufactured in the United States of America.

Notice

The information in this book is designed to help you make decisions regarding golf training. It is not intended as a substitute for professional fitness instruction and medical advice. You should seek your doctor's approval before beginning any fitness or diet program.

Contents

Acknowledgments

You might say that the seeds for this book were planted thirty years ago when my father, Robert Dine, first put a golf club in my hands. As a golf lover and student of the game, my dad taught me so much of what I know, and I hope that his meticulous attention to the fundamentals of the game shines through in this book. Sadly, my dad has now passed and will never see this book, but I know he's been with me every step of the way.

While my dad was a tremendous source of golf knowledge, I credit my mother, Jill, for my unbreakable positive attitude. She is my hero and role model as a wife and mother. I am blessed to have such wonderful parents, who show by example what unconditional love is all about. I thank you both for encouraging me to live with passion and to never accept any limits in my life.

In my three decades as a student and teacher of this game, I have met many wonderful people who have in some way contributed to this book. I must thank my golf coaches—Dole Cole at Abington Heights High School, and Mary Kennedy and Denise St. Pierre at Penn State—and my sport science professors at Penn State. Furthermore, each of the thousands of students I've worked with has helped contribute to my knowledge and teaching ability. We all have a different ideal swing to find, and in helping you find yours I become a more knowledgeable teacher of the game. I am also grateful for the LPGA for supporting me over the years and for creating the many top-shelf teaching development workshops. Lest I forget, my three brothers, Bob, Bill, and John—all of whom are accomplished golfers—offered their encouragement, love, and support throughout my years of chasing (and surpassing!) them in ability.

To my husband, Eric, I thank you for your love, encouragement, and boundless energy. If it weren't for your countless hours and book-writing knowledge, I doubt this project would have ever come to fruition. Furthermore, I can't imagine better synergy than what we have in sharing and adding to each other's knowledge of training for sports. Your expertise from the world of rock climbing helped shape much of this book's material on motor learning and mental training. It's been great to co-develop practice and training techniques that have helped so many people—in both our sports—improve their performance.

Many superior talents have contributed to the actual production of this book. Thanks to Laura Jorstad for copy editing, Eric McCallister for the stunning design, Rob Hörst for his excellent illustrations, and Tom McCarthy and Tom Ferrell for input and encouragement. I'm fortunate to teach at two excellent facilities—I thank Charlie and everyone else at Groff's Farm Golf Club, as well as Brad, Stan, Carol, and Red at Leisure Lanes Golf Center. Also, I am pleased to include photographs from several beautiful Lancaster area golf courses including Crossgates Golf Club, Four Seasons Golf Course, Groff's Farm Golf Club, and the Lancaster Country Club. And I must thank John Cunha, Sharon Hagenberger, and Gayle and Dave Plecha, for their lasting support of my golf endeavors.

Finally, I am deeply grateful for the love and support of Bob and Ethel Hörst— without your help it would be impossible for me to pursue my career as a dedicated golf pro while remaining focused on being an even more dedicated mother. And to my dear sons, Cameron and Jonathan—I love you both more than I can express, and I cherish every moment of your laughter and love.

Dedication

To my mother, Jill, for her unconditional love, friendship, and constant support. And in memory of my father, Robert Dine, for sharing his wisdom and love of life with me and for introducing me to the wonderful game of golf. Dad, I miss you more every year.

Introduction

Golf has entered a new era. Since the arrival of Tiger Woods in the late 1990s, record-sized tournament galleries have been spilling over onto driving ranges and courses. Men, women, and children from a wide range of backgrounds are picking up clubs and experiencing this glorious game. Finally the *gentleman's game* has become *everyone's game!*

Unfortunately, golf is difficult and not easily self-taught. The seemingly simple golf swing is in reality about as complex as sports skills get, and the odds of stumbling upon a good, effective golf swing through trial and error are about the same as winning the Powerball lottery. The real winning ticket is regular, long-term instruction from a veteran teaching professional. Next best is instruction from a good book or video grounded in the fundamentals of the game. The problem with these latter forms of instruction is that much of the material available is short on the important topics of what and how to practice most effectively, and quite long-winded on quick fixes, "stroke savers," and celebrity storytelling. While these books may entertain, they seem to have little real impact on the reader's performance. If the tens of thousands of books and videos sold each year are so effective, why are most golfers still scoring in the 100s? Did the last golf book or video you bought really change your game?

Golf Training will. If you resolve to consistently apply the principles and techniques contained here, you will improve—guaranteed! My confidence comes from success in working with thousands of golfers of all ages, sizes, and abilities. Any readers who fail to improve will do so because they were unwilling to let go of flawed practice methods and false notions about golf performance. As in all areas of life, improvement demands that you embrace change by letting go of the past and its ways, while engaging in new and more effective ways of thinking and acting.

For this reason, some low-handicap golfers may find this book to be every bit as challenging as will novice golfers. No, I won't advise an overhaul of your golf swing (that's rarely necessary anyway); I *will* recommend refinements of your current practice methods, however, as well as more empowering ways of thinking on the course. Consider it a reengineering of sorts, as together we will improve your golf performance using cutting-edge principles of motor learning, sport-specific fitness training, mental training, and sharpened dietary surveillance. You will begin playing better golf this season, while others enamored with old ways struggle to hang on to their current level of performance.

High-handicap and novice golfers have a different challenge—to believe implicitly in the principles described in this book and to apply the techniques consistently. Do so knowing that positive results, although not immediate, will come. In the coming months you will groove an effective swing—and with that foundation, there's no saying how good you will become in the seasons to follow. (I suspect far better than you can imagine!)

The *Golf Training* strategy unfolds in chapter 1 as I introduce you to eleven guiding principles of golf performance. These powerful principles lay the foundation for the rest of the book, and they should serve as the framework for your future training. Next, we'll evaluate your current strengths, weaknesses, goals, and level of commitment, because there can be no strategy for improvement until you know where you stand in each of these areas. Then you can step aboard the Cycle of Improvement and begin your journey to the best golf of your life.

Chapter 2 is a cutting-edge look into the principles of right practice as researched and proven by dozens of university studies in the field of motor learning and performance. If there is one chapter of this book that every golfer can learn something from, it's chapter 2. Presented here are a number of powerful practice strategies that have been proven to yield positive results with golfers of all ages and abilities. For many it will be a revelation to see that some of the tried-and-true traditional methods of golf practice are actually not effective for all golfers. You also will learn the hows and whys of some important learning techniques such as *blocked, variable,* and *random* practice, and you will be introduced to some relatively unknown concepts like that of *reminiscence.* Chances are some of the methods introduced in chapter 2 will be new to many golfers, despite the fact they've been used effectively by top professional athletes for years. Get ready to elevate the quality of your golf practice as you tap into twenty-first-century training techniques!

Chapters 3 through 5 provide basic swing instruction and proper technique for all the fundamental golf skills, from hitting your irons and woods to chipping and putting. Chapter 3 also includes an important section on correcting common swing errors that, if not nixed early on, could end up plaguing you for years. And since half the fun of golf is making great shots out of trouble, I'll teach you the techniques you'll need to get out of bunkers and rough, under trees, and more. Finally, I'll help you develop an effective preshot routine to anchor permanently your hard-earned skills.

The focus of chapter 6 is on winning golf's head games. Considering that the brain controls every decision and shot we make, it is the most important muscle to train. (For many golfers, it's unfortunately a muscle in atrophy due to years of neglect and mistraining.) Toward this end, I'll tee up several mental training techniques that you'll want to put to work today. I'll also present effective strategies for lowering pressure and tension, increasing motivation and confidence, relaxing more easily, improving poise, and learning to focus like a laser beam in the heat of competition or when everyone is watching on the first tee.

The book concludes with a look at two other subjects ignored by many golfers: fitness training and nutrition. First, I'll teach you some sport-specific exercises and stretches that hold the potential of enhancing your performance. No, these are not the standard chair stretches and office exercises—basically a waste of time—that are commonly featured in golf magazines. Instead they're highly effective exercises that, if performed on your days off, will help prevent off days due to injury or soreness. These exercises also promise to add yardage to your game and increase your endurance during the increasingly common five-hour round. Finally, I serve up a primer on nutrition and game-day diet for enhanced performance both on and off the links. The cliché is right: You *are* what you eat. Do you feel more like a nachos supreme or a sustained-energy Balance Bar? Top athletes in other sports know the impact diet has on performance, and it's time more golfers get the edge that performance nutrition provides. I'll show you the way.

Before you dive into chapter 1, I want to emphasize that practicing and playing golf should always be fun. As the old adage says, "Happiness and success are found in the journey, not the destination." As your personal golf trainer, then, I'm instructing you to take a few days (or weeks) off if your journey ever starts to feel joblike or stressful. A short break away from golf will renew your desire and can work wonders for your performance.

Finally, I want to tell you the biggest secret to better golf—it is to love the game unconditionally. Vow that any day you are outside swinging a club is a great day regardless of the results, and you will usually get the results you desire. Here's wishing you many wonderful days on the links. Have great fun and hole one in for me!

CHAPTER ONE

The Principles of Golf Training

1

I know of no more encouraging fact than the unquestionable ability of man to elevate his life by conscious endeavor.
—Henry David Thoreau

What is the difference between a golfer who shoots in the 70s or 80s and a high-handicap golfer scoring in the 100s? You might think it's genetic giftedness that tips the scales most heavily. Others would argue it is time and opportunity for practice. I've heard it uttered many times that "all the pros grew up on golf courses," or that "golf is more easily learned as a child than as an adult."

While there may be some truth to these statements, I believe just about anyone can become a low- to midhandicap golfer given the desire and an effective training program. Clearly, there is little shortage of desire in most people I meet at the driving range or course. It's the lack of effective training that proves to be their downfall. In fact, I would go so far as to say that some of the practice rituals I've observed produce no positive results at all.

You might be thinking, *I'm no ball beater—I train hard at the range.* But you have to consider whether your practice yields real improvement on the links. I'm not talking about a single personal-best round on your home course; instead, has your handicap or average score improved over your last ten rounds, or from year to year? For most people improvement is frustratingly slow or even negligible. In fact, some people come to me for instruction claiming they haven't improved noticeably in years, despite regular practice.

If any of this sounds familiar, don't be discouraged. The status quo can become history if you are willing to embrace some powerful how-to concepts, and then make the necessary changes in your training. The alternative is to keep doing what you're doing, in which case you will keep getting what you're getting. To me that sounds like a good definition of insanity—mindlessly doing the same things over and over, hoping to get different results.

Common Reasons for Lack of Improvement and Frustration

Regardless of your ability level, chances are you feel frustrated with your golf game at one time or another. (In fact, I'm sure a few tour pros feel this way each week.) Gaining awareness of flawed habits and beliefs, and learning to take intelligent actions to elevate your game is central to the *Golf Training* philosophy.

Listed below are ten barriers—or mental traps—that I see many golfers unknowingly encounter. Following each is the typical justification for continuing in this way. Do any sound familiar?

1. **Unwillingness to pay for professional instruction.** "I'd rather buy a new high-end driver than spend money on golf lessons."

2. **Practicing your strengths instead of your weaknesses.** "I don't want to look bad at the practice range."

3. **Blind obedience to antiquated or unproductive practice methods.** "I've always heard that hitting a bucket of balls with a single club is the best way of practicing."

4. **Inconsistent practice.** "If I practice every day this week, it doesn't matter that I didn't practice the last two weeks."

5. **Practicing too fast, too slow, or not enough.** "I feel like I have the best practices when I hit through two buckets of balls in a quick thirty-minute session."

6. **Fear of failure.** "I don't want to venture onto a golf course until I get better at the driving range."

7. **Not knowing your true weaknesses.** "My poor accuracy isn't a big problem because I can crush the ball farther than any player I know."

8. **Thinking too much.** "If I keep experimenting with my swing and swing thoughts, I know I will eventually improve my performance."

9. **Overemphasis on performance versus learning.** "I play the same course each week, so I have a better chance of scoring lower."

10. **Fear of change.** "I've always practiced this way: I hit half a bucket of balls with my driver and then a few balls with each of the rest of my clubs until the bucket is empty."

Now reread the list and circle the barriers that might be plaguing you. Summarize these problem areas into bullet points on an index card, and use this card as a bookmark while reading through this text. Constantly consult the card and think about how the material you read can help you overcome these handicaps and, in fact, lead you to more effective practice sessions and a higher level of performance on the links.

In this way, *Golf Training* is about restoring positive effects (and sanity) to your training. Though not common in a golfer's lexicon, I prefer the phrase *golf training* over *golf practice,* because improving your performance involves so much more than just hitting balls. Athletes in most other sports talk about *training* all the time, and I feel it's time that golfers embrace a training philosophy. Therefore, the pages that follow could be viewed as my manifesto regarding the need for golfers to embrace a new way of comprehensive *golf training*. Let's dig in deeper with a look the guiding principles of this program.

Eleven Guiding Principles of Golf Training

Eleven principles provide the foundation for this book. In the following chapters you'll see these principles give birth to a number of subprinciples as well as many extremely effective practice techniques. Ground your training in these absolutes to ensure maximum effectiveness and rapid improvement.

Principle 1: Golf is a game of near misses.

If you're looking for perfection, golf is the wrong sport. We've all observed golfers "at play" who display the attitude and demeanor of folks who won't be happy until they achieve perfection. Such characteristics produce tension and anxiety, which will always sabotage performance. And by even entertaining the prospect of perfection, you lay the groundwork for long-term disappointment and failure.

The practice tee is a microcosm of the course. Consider the golfer who keeps hitting and hitting with the same club and won't stop until he gets it exactly right. In most cases, his practice would be more effective if he logged shots with a variety of clubs instead of trying to stack balls with the single club. Ironically, perfectionism ensures mediocrity.

Remember, the perfect round of golf will never occur—it would require eighteen straight hole in ones! Begin to judge your performance in relative, not absolute, terms. If you're hitting more fairways and greens or making more 2-putts than ever before, that's a great sign of progress even if the day's score doesn't reflect it. Liberate yourself from perfectionism once and for all and train for competency in all facets of the game. Expect positive results—not perfection—and vow to always have fun no matter the situation. Great things will happen.

Principle 2: A good golf swing begins with a good setup.

The golf swing is a chain reaction event beginning from your setup position. Therefore, possessing a good setup (your grip, posture, and alignment) will give you a chance for the chain reaction to proceed in a correct, effective manner and produce an ideal result. With a poor setup, however, you have a greatly reduced chance of hitting an ideal shot—the quality of the chain reaction (your swing) is fundamentally doomed from the start.

You must also examine the quality of your entire preshot routine. Beginners typically have a mental checklist they go through that often evolves into a ritual lasting ten to twenty seconds or more. All the while tension builds, and soon even the best setup is compromised by the "paralysis by analysis." Likewise, experienced golfers often contemplate the ideal shot—or the importance of it—for too long. The end results are the same: tension, anxiety, and a less-than-ideal setup. Most golfers I work with benefit by condensing their pre-swing thoughts to a single key element, while turning the mechanics of the swing over to the subconscious mind for execution. The same is probably true for you.

The bottom line: Your setup is the paramount part of your swing. Thus, any search for the cause of gross errors (slice, hook, what have you) must always begin at the setup. If it's fundamentally sound, then you can proceed to the other stages of the chain reaction—the backswing, the force-producing downswing, and the follow-through—in the search for your swing error.

Principle 3: The swing path and orientation of the clubface at impact is more important than the size or speed of the swing.

The golf club is a tool that can be used effectively or ineffectively. It has a "sweet spot" in the center of the clubface where all the physics of design come together, making the golf ball jump off the clubhead like a Super Ball. The real secret of great golfers like Tiger Woods and Annika Sorenstam is their high percentage of center-face hits. Conversely, the typical amateur spreads hits around the clubface—some off the toe, some near the heel, some off the bottom edge, and the occasional great shot off the center face.

To increase the frequency of center-face hits, you need to gain more control of your club and groove a good, consistent swing path. The natural tendency in golf to overswing works contrary to this goal and can produce some wild results. It's like my occasional attempt to hammer in a nail when working around the house. The first few big, wild swings barely make contact, and the edge hits bend the nail off to one side. If I try again with a nice and easy half swing, though, I finally make center-face contact onto the nail, producing amazing power despite the lighter swing.

The golf swing is the same. Cut back to what feels like a three-quarter swing and you will regain control and increase accuracy as you begin utilizing the best part of the clubface. For most people, shot quality and consistency increase immediately, albeit with a slight decrease in distance. But that's a great trade-off if your goal is scoring lower! In time, your new and refined swing path will groove, and you will naturally begin taking bigger swings. Your distance will increase without a drop-off in quality.

The next time you struggle to make ball contact (or even whiff like I do with my hammer), think of my nail story and take a smaller swing. It may be the simplest, most effective correction for the average golfer.

Principle 4: Execution of a successful shot must be preceded by visualization of, and belief in, a successful shot.

All peak performers, whether in sports, business, or the performing arts, know the immense power of visualization. Although it does not absolutely ensure the ideal outcome, it does, based on your degree of preparation and training, move the odds firmly into your favor. This is especially true in a sport such as golf, which tests you many times during the course of a round or tournament. The edge gained through consistent visualization of the desired outcome is remarkable.

Visualization works by preparing a mental blueprint for action and outcome and, thus, the framework for reality. It must be factual, detailed, and positive if it is to give birth to the desired results. Certainly, many failures have been preprogrammed by poor-quality visualization based on erroneous information, negative thoughts, and unreasonable fears. Only through daily use in a wide range of applications will you master this skill.

Begin using visualization before every important action, whether a task at work or a fix-up at home. Create a full-color mental movie of the best course of action, and always end it with a vivid image of the ideal outcome. Use visualization before every golf shot, whether on the practice green or at the range, and from the first tee to the final putt on the course. Vividly visualize the exact shot you want to make, and it's more likely to occur in reality!

Manage tension proactively to elevate performance from tee to green.

Principle 5: Tension kills "feel" and, thus, the golf swing.

An artist needs to be able to "feel" the tip of his paintbrush with every stroke. A surgeon must have a precision "feel" for her scalpel. Likewise, golfers need a sensitive "feel" for their instrument if they are to perform up to par. Unfortunately, feel is not something easily taught, but rather fostered. The first step toward developing feel is learning to control tension.

Tension is the by-product of a wide range of things we encounter in our daily lives and on the golf course. For instance, getting caught in a traffic jam on the way to work can make you tense, as can getting caught in a fairway bunker. When you are tense and nervous, it's difficult to attain peak performance. In the examples above, the tension may result in a bad day at work or a bad day on the links, respectively.

The key to controlling tension is acute self-awareness. Staying aware of the thoughts and situations that make you tense empowers you to gain control over them. If you can't avoid a tense situation you've diagnosed, you can at least anticipate it ahead of time and counter it before it gets out of hand (say, as you walk over to make a bunker shot). Chapter 6 will introduce you to two methods of dealing with such tense situations.

Principle 6: Golf skills are specific to the parameters of the lie (ball up or down, grass length, up- or downhill position, quality of stance, and so on) and the overall setting.

In the science of motor learning, the idea of transference relates to how well the skills learned in the practice setting transfer to the performance setting. It has been demonstrated in numerous studies that transfer of skill drops off rapidly with even small differences between practice and performance conditions. This explains why hitting balls off a mat at the driving range transfers poorly to hitting off the widely varying surfaces of a golf course. Golf skills are very sensitive (specific) to the infinite variations of the playing field, and therefore must be practiced under highly variable conditions.

Top players perform well in almost any situation and at most courses. They do so because of their devotion to varying the practice conditions every day and, if possible, with every shot. One way tour pros do this is by playing a different course every week. Granted, you probably don't have the time to play fifty different courses a year like the pros do. Still, you can use your creativity to produce a wide range of reasonable lies on the grass at the range, and then on weekends travel to courses other than your home field. You'll learn in chapter 2 that the more time you log on different courses, and the greater the variation you introduce into your practice conditions, the better you'll play in the many unique settings you're sure to run into when it counts.

Principle 7: Training to correct weaknesses is the most effective way to practice.

This absolute might seem obvious, but it surprises me how many people practice in a manner contrary to it. Hitting a hundred perfect shots during practice is gratifying, but it is not effective practice if there's even a single bad club in your bag.

Practice sessions are for correcting your weaknesses and for expanding the use of newly acquired skills over a wider range of conditions. This means you'll be hitting a higher percentage of bad shots than people practicing their good clubs, but you'll become a better golfer for it. As hard as it may be, keep your ego out of your golf practice and commit to working on your weaknesses no matter how bad you might look. View bad shots as part of the learning process and a sign that you are serious about playing better golf. Meanwhile the "drive-for-show" ball beaters can continue practicing themselves into mediocrity.

Principle 8: The short game accounts for more than half the score and must, therefore, make up at least half your practice time.

It seems everyone knows that 60 percent of your shots are made within sixty yards of the hole. Why then do most golfers spend so much time practicing full-swing shots with their irons and woods while all but ignoring the crucial skills of chipping, pitching, putting, and bunker play? Ironically, the short-game skills are some of the easiest to learn if you simply make the effort. In fact, compared to learning to hit a driver, the short-game skills are downright easy to dial in!

It would be foolish not to spend at least half your practice time on the short game—that is, unless you're not losing any strokes around the green. Commit to dedicated weekly practice of the short game and you'll carve more strokes off your handicap than you would spending twice the amount of time hitting your driver. Beginners should focus whole practice sessions on just one or two aspects of the game—chipping and putting, pitch shots and bunker play, or full-swing shots with irons and woods. Experienced golfers who are competent in the all the basic skills must use a different approach. Although I'll address this subject in detail next chapter, their practice should consist of a random mix of skills during every session. Of course, about 60 percent of this practice time is focused on the short game.

Principle 9: Strength training must be sport-specific to improve clubhead speed and carry distance.

Strength training is the latest rage in golf, especially with the three-hundred-plus-yard drivers like Davis Love III and Tiger Woods crushing the ball on TV each weekend. Still, just as the efficacy of skill practice depends on its specificity to real-world use, so does strength training for a stronger swing.

Research in swing sports shows little transfer of strength gains from traditional gym training exercises (bench press, biceps curls, and the like) to the force of the swing. Only training that incorporates part, or all, of the actual movement will appreciably increase your swing strength. Something else to consider before you start pumping iron is that precise technique plays a far more important role in determining shot distance than does pure strength. If you are still struggling with the swing, your training time is better spent with a pro at the range than with a trainer in the gym.

Finally, I want to emphasize that general, all-around fitness training will improve your endurance on the course, enhance your quality of thinking, and reduce the risk of injury. The lower back and elbows are two common sites of injury that can be effectively protected given some modest strength training. See chapter 7 for these details as well as other tips for improving the quality of your health and golf fitness.

Principle 10: Club fit is more important than club brand name.

Having the latest, greatest technology matters only if you have mastered every technical aspect of the game. Thus professional golfers benefit most from all the super-high-tech equipment, while the average golfer mainly gets a lighter wallet.

The main equipment issue for most golfers should be correct club fit. Too many people are playing with poorly fitted clubs (grip size, weight, length, and lie) because they were bought off the rack from an unknowledgeable salesperson or because they are hand-me-downs. Since golfers come in all shapes and sizes, why shouldn't their clubs? There's no way every person can get perfect fit from the handful of sizes available off the rack. Good golf shops offer custom fitting of clubs, so call around and ask specifically for this service.

In the long run there are a lot of better places to spend your money than on the "must-have" cutting-edge clubs. Custom-fit clubs, professional instruction, and travel to many different courses are at the top the list.

Principle 11: Professional golf instruction is the optimal method of learning.

No book, video, or stack of magazines can provide the quality and personalized instruction of a top-notch teaching professional. Golf literature can be entertaining and extremely motivating, but it's almost impossible to sort through it all and determine the key item that will turn your game around. Self-instruction and trial-and-error learning are just too slow for anyone serious and passionate about golf.

Find a good teaching pro and your game will change forever. In a single lesson, a pro can identify the one or two critical errors in your swing (if that's your problem) and get you moving in the right direction. But don't stop there; get instruction on the other facets of the game—from putting to bunker play to course management. I suggest a minimum of five lessons for anyone scoring over 90 and no longer realizing any improvement. Novice golfers often need ten or more lessons spread out over the course of a season. Even low-handicap golfers should have a pro evaluate their game every season to determine what aspects of their performance could be tweaked in order to drop a few more strokes.

The best way to locate an effective teaching pro is by asking around at local golf shops or a public driving range. Look for a consensus of opinion about which local pro has produced the best results with the widest range of students. It's not always the pro at the largest facility or with the biggest name. Check the LPGA or PGA Web sites for a list of nearby teaching pros.

When you think you've identified a good professional, sign up for a single lesson and see if your teacher does the following:

1. Asks what your goals are.

2. Watches a series of swings before making any comments.

The golf swing is complex and not easily self-taught. One-on-one professional instruction is the paramount method of learning.

3. Inspects your setup (grip, posture, and alignment) before making changes to other parts of your swing.

4. Suggests just a few changes during the first lesson, as opposed to reworking your complete swing.

5. Points out the good aspects of your swing in addition to the problems.

6. Gives you (and hopefully writes down) one or two key swing thoughts and a few drills to take home from the lesson.

7. Explains some of the basic swing mechanics as well as pointing out the causes of your gross errors (slice, shank, and so forth).

8. Increases your confidence and motivation, as opposed to breaking your spirit with constant negative feedback.

If you answered yes to all these questions, chances are good you've found someone worth adopting as your long-term coach!

Finally, what is a fair rate for professional instruction? If the teacher passes the above test and produces positive results in your game, a series of five lessons is worth at least as much as the most expensive club in your bag.

Eleven Guiding Principles of Golf Training

Principle 1:	Golf is a game of near misses.
Principle 2:	A good golf swing begins with a good setup.
Principle 3:	The swing path and orientation of the clubface at impact is more important than the size or speed of the swing.
Principle 4:	Execution of a successful shot must be preceded by visualization of, and belief in, a successful shot.
Principle 5:	Tension kills "feel" and, thus, the golf swing.
Principle 6:	Golf skills are specific to the parameters of the lie and the overall setting.
Principle 7:	Training to correct weaknesses is the most effective way to practice.
Principle 8:	The short game accounts for more than half the score and must, therefore, make up at least half your practice time.
Principle 9:	Strength training must be sport-specific to improve clubhead speed and carry distance.
Principle 10:	Club fit is more important than club brand name.
Principle 11:	Professional golf instruction is the optimal method of learning.

Evaluating Your Performance and Setting Goals for Improvement

Your quest for a higher level of performance must incorporate constant evaluation and reevaluation to determine your strengths, weaknesses, desires, and level of commitment. Strengths are easy to sort out because it's human nature to think about and practice the things which you're good at. Identifying weaknesses is more difficult, because they aren't always as obvious as "I can't hit my driver." Listing your weak points probably doesn't score too high on the fun scale, either, but it is a necessity if you are going to continue improving in this difficult sport. Too many golfers waste precious years thinking about and practicing only the things they excel at, while unaware of how much the ball-and-chain of their weaknesses is holding them back.

Evaluate your game regularly to determine your true weaknesses—they are the key to a lower score.

The best way to identify your weaknesses is by asking yourself a series of detailed questions. Begin with a mental review of your last few rounds of golf. Ask yourself questions like: *What type of shots cost me the most strokes? Did tension increase throughout the round? Did I take too many chancy shots? Did I spend more time in the rough than on the fairway, and if so, why?* Regularly grilling yourself like this gives a very real view of your weaknesses—a view you may otherwise block out by always thinking about the next round, at the expense of never looking back for some constructive self-criticism.

Evaluating Your Game

During your next three rounds, keep track of the following statistics:

1. *How many fairways did I hit?*

2. *How many greens did I reach in regulation?*

3. *What's my average number of putts per hole?*

4. *How many penalty strokes did I incur and what was the cause of each?*

Use this knowledge to develop the most intelligent golf training practice strategy. For instance, if you make 70 percent of greens in regulation but average 3.5 putts per hole, it would be best to invest more practice time on the putting green than at the practice range.

Next, I suggest you have a local teaching professional observe as much of your game as possible. While beginners need the pro to check out all the basic swing skills, advanced golfers can often benefit most by hiring the pro for a playing lesson. The driving range can be too artificial a setting to accurately evaluate the weaknesses of mid- and low-handicap players, since their problems may be more mind- or strategy-related than mechanical.

Furthermore, some fundamental mistakes and weaknesses are subtle and not easily observed, even on the course. For instance, internal problems such as excessive tension, poor visualization, and high anxiety are difficult for an instructor to diagnose. This is where a self-assessment test comes in handy. Such a test, consisting of a series of introspective questions, takes the white light of your golf performance and breaks it into a spectrum of colors representing specific skills and attributes. It highlights your strengths and weaknesses and may even reveal your Achilles' heel. Only then can you develop a truly effective training program.

Take the Self-Assessment Test that follows. Read each question once and immediately answer it based on your most recent experience on the course first, and at the range second. Don't read anything into the questions or try to figure out their focus or "best" answer. I also urge you not to compare your score with anyone else. Such a comparison is meaningless, since we all hold ourselves to different standards when taking such self-assessment tests.

Self-Assessment Test

Score yourself between 1 and 5 on the following questions. Use this key for your response:

1 = Almost always   **4** = Seldom
2 = Often   **5** = Never
3 = Sometimes

1. I struggle to make a good turn on my backswing.

   1   2   3   4   5

2. At the range I hit my good clubs more than my problem clubs.

   1   2   3   4   5

3. I get anxious and tight when I address the ball on the course.

   1   2   3   4   5

4. I get a sore elbow when I practice or play regularly.

   1   2   3   4   5

5. On the course, I attempt to hit clubs that I have not practiced extensively and don't have a reasonable rate of success with.

   1   2   3   4   5

6. I get nervous and hit into obvious hazards, despite the fact that I have the skill and distance to make the same shot regularly in a practice setting.

   1   2   3   4   5

7. My lower back gets tight and sore late in a round of golf (or the morning after).

   1   2   3   4   5

8. The clubs I hit well at the range abandon me when I'm on the golf course.

   1   2   3   4   5

9. If I begin playing well on the course, my game falls apart before the end of the round.

   1   2   3   4   5

10. I get so physically drained during a round that my play on the back nine suffers.

   1   2   3   4   5

11. I lose my balance on full-swing shots.

   1   2   3   4   5

12. I fail to visualize the exact shot I want to make as I address the ball.

   1   2   3   4   5

13. Even if I'm tired and/or sore, I force myself to practice.

   1   2   3   4   5

14. I go a full week without practicing my putting.

   1   2   3   4   5

15. When I experience major problems, I try to self-diagnose them instead of consulting a teaching professional.

   1   2   3   4   5

16. I often go a week straight without playing, practicing, or performing any sport-specific drills.

   1   2   3   4   5

17. I struggle to reach greens in regulation.

   1   2   3   4   5

18. I get nervous and play worse when people outside my group are watching.

   1   2   3   4   5

Calculate Your Score in the Three Focus Areas

Transfer your score for each question onto the table on page 20. As you do, notice that each question represents a physical, technical, or mental/tactical skill. A perfect score would be 30 points in all three areas of focus. However, since the goal of this assessment is identifying weaknesses, you should be most interested in your lowest-scoring questions and focus area. First, take note of your lowest-scoring focus area—is it physical, technical, or mental? Now circle the six or eight lowest-scoring questions and condense these problem areas into bullet points on an index card. These points must be the target of your golf training, and I promise you that the key to improving in each can be found in the pages of this book. Keep this index card handy and take notes as you keep reading.

Physical Questions	Technical Questions	Mental Questions
Q1: _____	Q2: _____	Q3: _____
Q4: _____	Q5: _____	Q6: _____
Q7: _____	Q8: _____	Q9: _____
Q10: _____	Q11: _____	Q12: _____
Q13: _____	Q14: _____	Q15: _____
Q16: _____	Q17: _____	Q18: _____
Total: _____	Total: _____	Total: _____

The Cycle of Improvement

Your completed Self-Assessment is your "boarding pass" to the Cycle of Improvement. This is a process cycle with three stages: set goals, take action, and assess results. Thanks to your Self-Assessment, you can strategize goals that meet your weaknesses head-on. Only then will your actions (practice) be properly aligned to bring about the positive change you desire.

A successful trip around the Cycle gives birth to a new level of performance based on the more skilled "new you." The Cycle of Improvement, in fact, becomes a spiral of improvement, with continual reevaluation revealing new problem areas hindering further improvement. Of course, the reevaluation must give birth to new goals, followed by new actions, which will produce more exciting results.

One trip around the Cycle may take anywhere from a few weeks to a season, depending on your desires, commitment, and skill level. Signs that you have completed the Cycle include: a plateau in performance, training that's beginning to feel "flat," and possibly a drop in motivation. If you experience these signs, take a few days off, consider retaking the Self-Assessment, and schedule a meeting or playing lessons with your teaching pro. But keep the Cycle going and always know where you stand. If you don't, the quality of your practice and performance, as well as your motivation, will level off or even collapse into a downward spiral. Getting stuck on or skipping over one stage of the process is the reason many people stagnate in this sport (or in business or life, for that matter).

Goal Setting

Most people set goals in the long term—to break 100 or shoot scratch, to win a tournament or maybe play some dream course. But to set only long-term goals is to miss the boat to them altogether. In fact, short-term goals are what fuel and steer your boat toward long-term destinations. Start your trek today by establishing some written goals in three time frames: short term (daily), medium term (weekly and monthly), and long term (multiyear or lifetime).

Short-term goals are simply a daily to-do list specific to improving your golf performance. Write them down the night before or as you eat breakfast in the morning, then don't let the day end without completing the list. Here are a few examples. If you are planning a session at the range, set goals specific to training your weaknesses and expanding use of recently acquired skills. If you're headed to the gym, write down all the sport-specific stretches and exercises you plan to perform. If a round of golf is in the day's plan, write down exactly the stretches and warm-up shots you need to complete to put yourself in peak form before teeing off. (This way you'll be sure to allow enough time for a nonrushed preparation.) No matter what the task, a written list—whether on a Post-it note or in a training log—is the carrot that compels consistent, intelligent actions.

Medium-term planning integrates your training and golfing schedule with the rest of your life. It will optimize your use of time and keep you on the fast track to higher performance. Loosely plan things out on a calendar a few weeks or months in advance. First mark big events such as tournaments, important outings, work and family obligations, and so forth. Now pencil in a proposed practice and playing schedule that contains no stretch of more than two days without some form of golf training or actual play. Consistency is everything, and advance planning is the only way to make sure you'll fit in the volume of practice sessions you need.

When all the important items are in place, the many less important things in life can fall in where time allows. I'm talking about the myriad distractions vying for your attention and time—television, social outings, surfing the Net, and so forth. Although it's easy to be lured by the instant gratification they offer, short- and medium-term planning will help keep you on track toward more lofty, meaningful accomplishments.

Finally, there are the long-term "mega goals" floating around in your mind. This might be the ultimate score you'd like to achieve, or a dream course you'd like to play. If there's any chance for them to ever become reality, you must remove them from the realm of fantasy and put them down in black and white. There's a magical power in writing things down. It creates a magnetic pull toward the goal— as if what you want, wants you!

Set Your Goals

Detailed goals compel consistent daily action in high-value areas—and if you're reading this book, golf is one such area for you. Ask yourself, *What can I do in the next hour, day, week, or month to enhance my golf performance?* Set short-, medium-, and long-term goals accordingly. Get busy, and enjoy the journey!

Short-term goals: _____

_____

Medium-term goals: _____

_____

Long-term or lifetime goals: _____

_____

Discipline and Desire: The Great Equalizers

Excellence in anything—sports, business, relationships—takes a lot of discipline. Discipline to do all the things that point toward your goal and discipline to abstain from the things that will move you away from it. When it comes to discipline, there's no secret formula or strategy to talk about; it simply comes down to how badly you want it.

There are many talented golfers who never live up to their potential because they lack discipline—for every two steps forward they take at least one step back. Conversely, many golfers of average talent have become great because they cut ties to anything that might hold them back. In the long run they realized their full potential.

Discipline alone does not guarantee success, but the lack of it goes a long way toward guaranteeing that you will fall short of your potential. Considering your current skill level, is your degree of discipline and desire honestly high enough to move you toward your goals? If not, you must either increase your discipline and ignite your desire, or scale back your long-term goals. I hope you will do the former and advance confidently toward the best golf of your life.

Training Tip

Discipline is fundamental in the pursuit of excellence. When planning how to spend your time, it's vital to distinguish between high-value, goal-directed activities and low-value "filler" activities. Favor activities and practices that will carry you toward your goals, and ignore what other people are doing. Thoughtfully acting in self-directed, goal-oriented ways is the key to a higher level of golf performance (and living).

CHAPTER TWO

The Secrets to Effective Practice

2

Knowing is not enough; we must apply. Willing is not enough; we must do. —Johann Wolfgang Von Goethe

This chapter could be called "the fork in the road" because it presents you with two alternatives. After reading it, you will either continue to practice as you always have and reap similar results, or you will take a chance and embark on a new stratagem. The safe road offers the security of continuing in the comfort zone of familiar workouts and known results (or lack thereof). The new path will bring you many challenges and fear of the unknown, but it also leads to more effective practice and a higher level of golf performance. It's your decision—status quo or handicap low!

The principles and training methods in this chapter are deeply rooted in the rapidly expanding field known as motor learning and performance. As a golf professional with a degree in kinesiology, I thought it critical to incorporate the powerful motor learning concepts into my golf instruction. Dozens of university studies in this field have shown clearly the ineffectiveness of certain practice schemes held dear by many athletes, including golfers. In fact, a certain practice method popular with some golfers can produce negative results on the golf course (more on this in a bit). These studies unveiled many new and highly effective ways to practice, which I will introduce to you on the pages to follow.

Finally, I want to point out a common theme of motor learning studies that you need to be aware of: Changing your standard practice regimen to one with which you are unfamiliar will result in a drop-off in your apparent competency during practice. This decline in practice-day performance is a sign you're stretching the bounds of your abilities—just what you need to do if practice is to be effective. So stay the course, despite an initial increase in mis-hits and potential public embarrassment. Remember, your actual abilities on the golf course are what count, and the challenges of the new practice regimen are moving you toward that goal.

Every time you pick up a golf club, it is vital to decide whether you're swinging for *practice* or *performance*. I cannot overstate the importance of this simple concept of focus, especially considering the number of golfers I see performing at the range each day. Practice is about working on your weaknesses in the most effective way, and not about being a ball-hitting robot with your best club.

On that note, let's jump into a short course on motor learning and performance in which I will discuss ten important concepts guaranteed to accelerate your learning of golf skills and maximize your performance on the course.

What to Practice and How Much to Practice

This first question has an easy answer: your weaknesses! Having completed the Self-Assessment Test in chapter 1, you should be well aware of your area of general weakness (physical, technical, or mental), as well as some of your more specific problems. Then there are the obvious weaknesses of the clubs you can't hit, and the ones that produce inconsistent results.

Arrange your weak items into a list beginning with those that cost you the most strokes and ending with the weaknesses only an advanced golfer would need to worry about. For instance, putting, pitching, bunker shots, and middle irons are critical items that should be given a high priority, while driver, 2-iron, or any trick shots (draws, hooks, and the like) should be near the bottom of the list. Focusing your daily practice on the high-priority items puts you on the fast track to a lower score. The bottom-of-list items like "learning to hit my drive" are better viewed as long-term goals.

As to the frequently asked question of *How much practice time is best?*—there is no simple answer. It depends on a number of factors, including your current skill level, overall physical fitness, desire, and long-term goals. As a rule, highly skilled golfers need to invest an exceedingly large amount of time to realize even the slightest increases in ability. Accordingly, many pros spend upward of eight hours a day, six days per week on the job (playing, practicing, and working out). Conversely, beginners can improve with as little as one hour of practice, three days per week.

Next, consider your overall fitness level, because golf does place some rather unusual and potentially injurious strains on your body. If you work a sedentary job, have a history of injuries, or are out of shape, overweight, or of advanced age, you are at risk for a golf-related injury. While I will address fitness training thoroughly in chapter 7, let me point out that if you are in one of the above categories you should spend up to half your golf training time on improving your physical fitness.

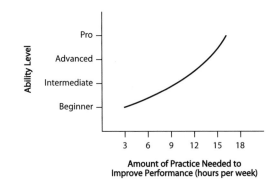

Practice Time Needed to Improve

Amount of Practice Needed to Improve Performance (hours per week)

For instance, if you have eight hours per week for golf training, spend four hours at the gym doing aerobic and strength training and just four hours actually practicing golf skills. Although the reduced skill training time will mean a slower rate of learning golf skills, the investment in fitness training lowers your chances of missing weeks or months of practice due to injury. More important, consistent fitness training will add to your longevity in this sport and improve the overall quality of your life.

Even if you are physically fit, motor learning studies have shown there is a limit to how much practice is effective. In terms of continuous practice, it seems about two hours is the outer limit for receiving added benefit from a session. Thus, advanced golfers with long practice days need to break up training into several parts each lasting one to two hours. For the amateur golfer practicing after work and on weekends, I suggest single sessions of between forty-five and ninety minutes, three to six days per week. Consider three, forty-five-minute practice sessions as the bare minimum; anything less serves as only a maintenance schedule.

It should now be obvious (if it wasn't already) that the average recreational golfer will spend but a fraction of the time practicing that a pro would. More than the pro golfer, then, your practice must be highly focused and effective, with no wasted time. I call it "training smart." The rest of this chapter serves up many smart bombs for your training arsenal.

Training Tip

Optimal, not maximal, practice is the goal. Novices should begin with three, one-hour sessions per week, building toward three to five, sixty- to ninety-minute session per week as skills improve. Advanced golfers may need two hours or more, six days per week, to realize further improvements.

Learning New Skills

Your body learns and remembers motor skills such as the golf swing by building detailed motor performance maps or *schemas* in the nervous system and brain. It has been shown that new schemas are developed better during the early portion of your practice session while the body and mind are fresh. Increasing fatigue, anxiety, or rushing through your practice session translates to slow, maybe even no, learning of new skills.

After completing a warm-up of stretching and fifteen to twenty practice shots with a couple of your good clubs, proceed straight to work on your top-of-the-list weaknesses. One day it might be wedge play, the next workout it might be long irons; but whatever it is, spend this most valuable middle portion of your session building your schemas. It's now or never for teaching your nervous system new skills and grooving the swing of a new club. Get to it early!

Ironically, many golfers tend to hit through all their good clubs first, and only then move on to the problem areas when there are only a few balls or minutes left to practice. At my golf center, which includes a practice bunker and putting area, the vast majority of golfers head straight to the practice tee, only to finish up with a few minutes in the bunker or on the green. They do this despite the fact that sand play and putting are major areas of weakness for most amateur golfers. As explained above, such end-of-workout practice of problem skills has little benefit. Conversely, the later part of your workout is the ideal time to fortify skills you already possess to a high level. Plan to conclude your session by practicing some of your best skills despite the fact you might feel fatigued and lacking in sharpness.

Let's consider the situation in which you arrive at the range already tired and tense from a rough day at work, or fatigued from another sport or gym workout. In this case, I urge you to forgo training new or weak skills, since a stressed nervous system will acquire few, if any, new schemas. Instead, use this situation to work on awareness and management of the tension at hand, while practicing with the clubs and skills with which you are already competent. Called "fatigued skill practice," this is normally incorporated toward the end of a practice when fatigue is high. The athlete (or team) practices known skills (or plays) requiring skill recall, but no new skill learning. This recall, in the less-than-ideal performance state, increases command and control of a skill, yielding greater reliability in stressful situations, whether that means the heat of competition or the heat of the midday sun.

Training Tip

Blocked Practice

Blocked practice—identical repetitions of a skill—is the most popular practice method in a variety of sports, including gymnastics and golf. Isolating and practicing repeatedly a single difficult gymnastic move is an example of blocked practice, as is hitting five consecutive shots (or a bucket of balls, for that matter) with a single club from the same lie.

Misuse of blocked practice is extraordinarily common among golfers and can have negative effects on performance. In fact, this misuse is the number one cause of the *my-skills-left-me-on-the-course* phenomenon experienced by many amateur players who seem to hit so well at the range. Let's sort things out.

Blocked, repetitive practice of a new skill will produce rapid positive results. For instance, if you perform the same long putt three times in a row, each putt should get better, as should your feel for that specific spot on the green. The same is true if you are practicing 5-iron shots off a mat at the range. Repeated identical attempts will yield improvement over the course of many trials. This is explained by the fact that on the first trial your nervous system had to guess at the proper execution based on schemas from similar past situations, but on the second, third, and subsequent tries it only had to modify the known movements from prior attempts. This process results in an increasing sense of "feel" with each attempt.

A radical change is needed, however, once feel, some confidence, and a reasonable rate of success at a new skill have been developed. Further blocked reps have little value and can result in a false sense of confidence and poor use of the skill in settings different from that practiced. The classic example is hitting off mats at the range, which is tightly blocked by the perfect lie and stance each time. Many golfers have basked in the glory of their perfect iron shots off range mats, only to have their iron play evaporate on the highly variable surfaces of our playing field— the golf course. The swing may seem the same in both places, but the schemas may differ. When faced with anything other than a perfectly flat lie and stance—the kind you are used to from the practice mat—your performance will likely be inconsistent, and may be frustratingly poor.

This example shows that beyond the early stages of learning a skill, blocked practice is for blockheads! Once you've achieved a modest degree of success—let's say greater than 50 percent solid, straight shots with a given club—further real gains (those that won't leave you on the course) require variable and randomized practice.

Training Tip

Use blocked practice to accelerate learning during the initial trials of a new skill or skill position. Upon achieving a 50 percent success rate of solid hitting, reduce the amount of blocked practice in favor of variable or randomized practice. This will grow your golf skills most rapidly!

Variable Practice

As I explained in the previous section, it is not enough to acquire use of a skill in a single fixed setting. The ultimate goal is instant and proficient use of the skill in any novel situation you come upon, which, of course, happens all the time on the links. The tried and proven way to do this is with variable practice.

Suppose you've just acquired the skill to consistently hit a certain club from a

Distribution of Schemas

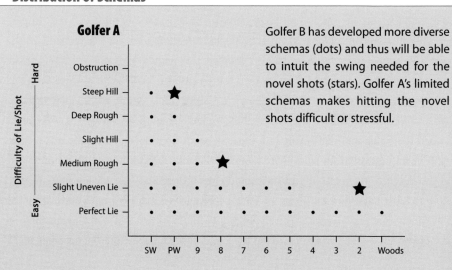

Golfer A

Golfer B has developed more diverse schemas (dots) and thus will be able to intuit the swing needed for the novel shots (stars). Golfer A's limited schemas makes hitting the novel shots difficult or stressful.

perfect stance and lie, such as off a mat or flat, well-kept grass at the range. To incorporate variable practice, then, you would practice the same shot but with constant variation of condition—on *every* shot. To do this you need to move onto a nonperfect grass surface with its lumps, divots, spots of thick turf, hardpan, and such. Since a unique schema is used for every different shot condition, the motor programs you developed for shots with perfect lies will not carry over well. Consequently, your shot quality will immediately drop off upon initiation of variable practice. Don't worry: This is good.

Studies have shown that the broad range of new schemas developed from variable practice is what allows for brilliant performances in widely varying situations like you'll find on a golf course. More exciting is that having solid and wide-ranging schemas for a given club enables your nervous system to approximate the correct solution for many novel situations you might come upon. This explains how the top tour players frequently pull off a miracle shot from the most unlikely position or lie, one they may have never encountered before. When asked about it afterward, the pros often comment about "using intuition" or "just letting the shot happen." But ultimately, it's their bountiful schemas (and the years of variable practice that develop them) that are to credit for the intuition and feel for the shot.

I cannot overstate the importance of variable practice for all but beginner golfers. Beyond the earliest successful trials of a new skill, blocked practice is a curse that will have you cursing on the course for years to come. Use your imagination to introduce realistic variation into the practice of your good clubs. Likewise, you must constantly vary your target, because golf is a target-oriented sport. Never hit more than a few similar shots in a row, and avoid hitting into a

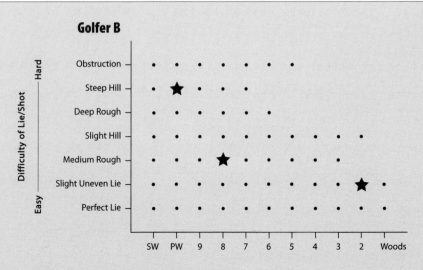

Practice from a wide range of lies and
positions to maximize your golf training.

no-target void. These rules apply to all types of golf shots, from putting to bunker play. Vary the conditions and the target regularly, and you'll be surprised by the stellar results on the links.

Training Tip

Variable practice expands the learning of newly acquired skills for use over a wide range of conditions and situations. Dump a pile of balls onto the grass, then just tap them out of the pile into a section of nonperfect grass and hit each ball from whatever lie you are left with. Also, change your target every few shots. Advanced golfers (or those at well-kept ranges) need to be more clever and create difficult lies by placing the ball in more difficult-to-hit positions. Of course, the gold standard for variable practice is playing a round of golf. It's for this reason that I encourage my students to "play to practice"—that is, play rounds of golf with the sole objective of working on shot making and without the pressure of keeping score.

Random Skill Practice

On the golf course you never hit two consecutive shots with the same club, except for perhaps after a mis-hit out of bounds or into water. In fact, consecutive shots are usually with significantly different clubs; you are likely to tee off with a long iron or wood, then take a second shot with a middle iron or wedge. Execution of these different skills requires rapid recall of dissimilar motor programs. If you are to be successful on the course, you need to practice this recall of skills during your training sessions.

Random practice is the proven method for training such recall of skills. It may be the most powerful practice method for developing the long-term retention of skills you need for a lifelong sport such as golf. Interestingly, random practice is yet another invaluable training tool I see too few golfers employing at the range.

Beyond the blocked practice of brand-new skills and the variable practice used to broaden application of newly acquired or inconsistent skills, random practice should rule. It's pretty simple. Never hit two consecutive shots with the same club or from the same lie, and keep the target changing throughout. Employ any club with which you hit reasonably well from a natural lie, and alternate between partial- and full-swing shots. Your goal is to mimic the recall of different skills as they might be called upon during a round. In fact, a fun way to maximize effectiveness of random practice is to pretend you are on the course actually

"Playing for practice" is a powerful golf training strategy for intermediate and advanced players.

playing. Visualize yourself on the tee and hit a single shot with your driver or a wood. Follow this with an iron shot and a chip shot as if you were playing a par-5 hole. Use of this powerful practice strategy will make you a master of skill recall when you arrive at the course for real.

Another advantage of random practice is development of the "one-chance" mental mode of shot making. On the course you obviously need the ability to step up to the ball and just let the swing unfold correctly the first time. Unfortunately, overuse of blocked practice at the range makes one-try shot making on the course the ultimate tension-producing event. The longer you stand over the ball contemplating the fact that *I have to get it right first try*, the lower the chances are that you will. If any of this sounds familiar, use of one-shot random practice will take several strokes off your game this season!

The amount of random practice you employ depends on your skill level. Novice golfers still learning to hit their first few clubs should use blocked practice exclusively and forget about random practice at this point. Intermediate golfers need roughly an equal mix of blocked practice of new skills, variable practice of working skills, and random practice of the solid clubs in the bag. Finally, highly skilled golfers who hit all their clubs with precision glean the most benefit from variable and random practice. In fact, the best place to get an infinite mix of both is on the golf course.

This concept gives birth to a crucial principle of golf performance: The greater your skill level (lower handicap), the more time you need to spend actually playing golf to realize further improvement. Driving ranges have definite limitations, and no matter how creative you are at using variable and random practice, you will never come close to simulating the huge variations you find on the course. Thus, the ultimate form of random practice is getting out and playing as many different courses as possible. While I do advise beginners to play the same executive course a number of times as an ice breaker, the comfort and familiarity of playing the same course all the time will stunt your growth and give a false sense of progress. What's more, playing many different courses develops your problem-solving, tactical, and mental skills. The choice is yours: Keep playing the same course in search of a better score there, or play a wide range of courses and become a better golfer everywhere.

Training Tip

Random practice of skills enhances functional use and long-term recall, and should be employed by all intermediate and advanced golfers. Playing a wide range of golf courses is the ultimate form of random practice, because it elevates both technical and cognitive skills. Thus, "playing as practice" is increasingly important as skill level increases.

Cue Words and Swing Thoughts

Cue words are powerful teaching aids, and they are commonly used in sports ranging from football to gymnastics to golf. They are the "tell" part of the classic "show-and-tell" instruction used by teaching professionals, and in my opinion far more important than the "show" in learning new skills.

A good golf instructor will find just the right cue words to help you understand, feel, and perform troublesome golf skills. If these cues don't connect with you and produce no improvement, ask your instructor for others. Cue words are categorized as *auditory, visual,* or *kinesthetic,* and the instructor might simply need to use words from another category to make them more instructional to you. For instance, part of the basic swing setup could be described visually with the cue phrase *let your arms hang straight to the ground,* or it could be explained kinesthetically with *relax and feel gravity extend your arms naturally.*

You can learn all facets of the game more quickly through use of these performance cues. Words or phrases such as *hit the sand two inches behind the ball and explode through it* or *putt through the ball* are far more powerful learning aids than simply observing and then trying to copy your instructor's perfect execution of the skill. If your pro is fond of saying "watch me" instead of giving you descriptive cues, then it's time to find another instructor.

While cue words are for learning, swing thoughts are for performing. Over time you must distill your litany of cue words down to one swing thought. Based on past experiences, pick a single cue word or phrase that has proven most effective for you.

While you can still go through a brief sequence of pre-swing thoughts during setup, you can only have a single thought as you initiate the swing. You will need to experiment to determine the best swing thought for each club or shot you make. For instance, you might find *pull with the left hand* to be the most effective cue during the downswing on iron shots, while for tee shots you might stay down longer by thinking *look for the tee to appear after impact.* Many more cue words will be offered in the following chapters, but by all means come up with your own. Keep them brief and simple, however—with swing thoughts, less is more.

Training Tip

Cue words and phrases enhance your understanding, learning, and recall of golf skills. Keep them concise, accurate, and specific to a given skill. Find unique cue words for each different skill you learn. Over time, reduce your cues to a single word or swing thought to direct the execution of each skill.

Self-Awareness and Error Detection

Self-awareness and error detection are two critical skills you hear too little about in this sport. I teach my students to develop these skills early on, because only through keen self-awareness will you master this sport.

During both play and practice, your thoughts, arousal level, tension, and focus are in a constant state of flux. As discussed earlier, anxiety and tension make motor learning difficult and peak performance impossible. Even worse, any learning that does take place will involve "mapping" of poor habits and techniques caused by your tense physique. In the end such practice time will be at best wasted time; at worst, it will produce negative results.

It's therefore vital to foster the habit of constantly monitoring the quality of your thoughts as well as your level of muscular tension. This awareness empowers you to better focus your thoughts and modulate your physiology to maintain an ideal state for learning and performing. Toward this end, I will provide you with several highly effective techniques for "Winning the Head Games" in chapter 6.

Similarly, error detection involves a self-evaluation of your actual performance, which in turn allows immediate correction of your swing from day to day or even shot to shot, if necessary. Because this requires an understanding of swing mechanics, I will serve up a crash course on this topic in the next chapter. Ideally, your golf pro should be the one teaching you basic mechanics. (If he or she isn't, ask!) That way you can continue to learn as you practice outside the pro's presence by making your own swing adjustments as needed. Of course, without some knowledge of mechanics the best you can do is trial-and-error adjustments, which is tantamount to shooting in the dark.

Error detection comes in two stages. Initially you will learn to interpret errors in the ball flight and adjust your grip, posture, alignment, or swing (whatever the probable cause) for the next shot. For high-handicap golfers, it's best to assess a mean error over a series of shots, and only then make a single change. Constant tweaking from shot to shot will ultimately turn into trial-and-error training, which is a waste of time.

Advanced golfers are a different breed. Their heightened sensory awareness allows immediate error detection upon impact with the ball. I'm sure you've seen countless examples of this on TV tour coverage, as a golfer winces or reacts on the follow-through to what surely is an errant shot. Such a well-developed kinesthetic sense will come to you in time, but vigilance at assessing the quality of the actual shot is still paramount to diagnosing mechanical problems.

Modern video and computer technology is what some might consider the ultimate in error detection. Slow-motion analysis and liberal use of the rewind button makes it easy to see for yourself even the slightest error. Such objective views of performance are powerful learning tools—but there is a minor downside to this technology. Commonly the analyst will play the tape of your swing next to that of a famous pro to illustrate basic differences in setup, swing plane, release, and such. The danger in this is the natural tendency of students to actually copy the swing of the pro instead of just adopting the fundamentals of his or her swing. Modeling the swing of a pro, whether from TV coverage or such a computer analysis, is unwise because few amateur golfers can maintain control of the typical "big," pro-like swing. In fact, most golfers I work with benefit most by taking less of a swing.

Training Tip

Constant self-awareness is essential for learning and improving skills, eliminating bad habits, and controlling tension. Only by monitoring the dynamic landscape of your mind and body can you make the tweaks necessary to maintain optimal performance. Likewise, strive to analyze each shot (or series of shots) to detect mechanical errors in your swing.

Visualize every shot before you pull the trigger.

Synergy of Mental and Physical Practice

Interlacing mental and physical practice will yield faster learning of sport skills than either one alone. For instance, if you aren't employing visualization before every golf shot or putt, you are surely lowering the efficacy of your practice. Although mental training will be covered in detail in chapter 6, I wanted to include a brief section here to stress its importance to effective practice.

The primary use of visualization in practice is to "see" the target, ideal flight path, and desired ball placement. Similarly, in putting you should visualize the perfect line or arc that the ball will travel to the hole. Create a visual movie before every shot or putt, always making the images as accurate, detailed, and vivid as possible. The better the imagery, the better the results. Therefore, it is vital that you develop the habit of visualizing every shot clearly before swinging.

As with physical skills, your mental abilities will improve with practice. Certainly it can be discouraging to beginners when that actual flight path or putt rarely matches their visualization of the shot. By staying the course and faithfully exercising your imagination in this way, however, the payoffs will eventually come. Remember that all successful athletes—whether it's Allen Iverson shooting a three or Serena Williams serving an ace—use visualization to maximize their performances. So should you.

Training Tip

Interlacing mental and physical practice produces greater results than physical practice alone. Visualize every shot—the flight path of the ball and the ideal outcome—before you swing in order to program the mind and body for accurate execution of the skill. Although you may not recognize the positive effects on any given shot, the aggregate effect will be higher shot quality and better overall performance.

Simulators and Mechanical Aids

Simulators are devices intended to emulate real-world tasks, ranging from flying a jet airliner to blocking a football player. In golf, simulators range from extremely pricey virtual golf courses to a five-dollar aluminum putting "hole" on the living room carpet. Ultimately, the value of such simulators must be gauged according to price, convenience, and realism. But since this chapter is about effective practice, it's the latter consideration that counts.

Realism is everything when it comes to assessing the transfer of simulator training to the actual task. Motor learning scientists have shown that the greater the similarity between the simulator and the task being simulated, the greater the transfer of learning. For instance, putting across a carpeted floor into a cup is not realistic beyond the setup and stroke itself. Nothing is learned regarding break and probably very little with respect to speed (is the speed of your carpet anywhere close to the greens you play on?). Therefore, this practice will transfer very little learning to real-world greens, and is basically a waste for all but beginners still learning setup, alignment, and stroke.

Another common putting simulator is the Astroturf "runway," complete with a few bumps along the way. This is slightly better because it's a bit more realistic. Still, unless you run into a green with the same arrangement of bumps, transfer of skill from practice will be small. The best putting simulator I've seen is the Electronic Putting Challenge by GL Technology. This computerized putting machine features seventy-two different six-foot putts with a wide variety of breaks and hills. Extraordinary realism means far greater transfer of learning to the real world. For a serious golfer, it's the only putting simulator worth buying, unless you can put a green in your backyard.

Virtual golfing is the latest rage at some golf shops because you can actually "play" Pebble Beach while in downtown Philadelphia! While these simulators are clearly entertaining, they possess minimal training value due to the fixed stance and lie. Such blocked practice is effective only for a beginner and, as discussed earlier in this chapter, can even hurt the game of more competent players. As a rule, dabble in these fixed-position simulators for fun, but forget using them regularly for practice.

As with simulators, there are many mechanical aids available that hold the promise of enhancing your performance. Such aids range from a variety of straps and braces to gimmicky, nontraditional clubs. As a rule, these devices can improve the performance of your practice by correcting some fundamental error in the swing. As stressed throughout this chapter, however, transfer of learning from practice to performance is very specific to the similarity of the feel and conditions. Therefore, you'll need to continue using the mechanical aid in the play setting to maintain the positive benefits it lends to your performance. Do you want to play the rest of your life with such a crutch?

The bottom line is this: Limited use of mechanical aids during the early stages of learning may help develop the kinesthetic sense of position, can improve certain elements of the swing, and may also help an experienced golfer unlearn ineffective motor programs that have been grooved in over a long period of time. In the end, however, you need to learn to perform a sound swing by yourself and without mechanical aid. This takes focus, determination, and lots of practice. Quick-fix technology rarely produces lasting results.

Training Tip

Simulators and mechanical aids are most useful for beginners learning basic posture, alignment, and skills. Most simulators, however, lack enough realism and provide too little variation to transfer to our playing field. The serious golfer is always better off choosing the real thing. Some mechanical aids can help in unlearning poor technique, but feel may be lost and your performance may drop when this crutch is removed.

The Reminiscence Effect

The single greatest handicap for serious golfers is thinking too much and trying too hard. While I love seeing excited, passionate people swinging the club, golf is a finesse sport requiring masterful control of the mind and body. Yes, learning the golf swing is difficult and certainly takes a lot of thought and effort.

Upon grooving the basic swing, however, you must decrease your thinking and let your motor skills take command. When done completely, this is called being "in the zone." The opposite of being in the zone—and, unfortunately more common among golfers who stand over the ball too long—is "paralysis by analysis."

Reminiscence is a fascinating phenomenon characterized by more centered, intuitive play after a rest period of a few days to a few weeks away from golf. Athletes in skill sports often experience reminiscence, though, it may be most noticeable among golfers. This experience of performing better after a break away from practice and play results from the fact that your body and subconscious mind remember more about complex skills (the motor programs or schemas you've developed) than your conscious mind. In the midst of a golf season you may find yourself at the point of trying too hard, overanalyzing everything, and focusing too much on the outcome of each swing. Your well-honed swing may begin to feel awkward and forced, and your performance may plateau or begin to drop off despite large amounts of practice.

Taking a week or two off will clear your head and, more important, reset your intuitive sense of the golf swing. After your layoff, skills will be more automatic and again feel natural as your body remembers (reminisces) its well-learned motor skills. This "try-softer" style will not overpower your body's knowledge of skills as did the old try-harder approach. You'll be pleasantly surprised to find yourself golfing better, more efficiently, and with more flow than before. You just might enter the zone and shoot a personal-best round or win a tournament after taking some time off. Tiger Woods did just this in 1997 when he won three tournaments—including his record win at the Masters—after taking a week off from tournament play before each event. That was reminiscence at work!

Training Tip

If you are practicing hard (or playing a lot) but only getting worse, it's time to take a few weeks off and let your skills resurface thanks to reminiscence. Don't even think about golf for a week or two, and you'll come back swinging better than ever. You may also experience the powerful reminiscence effect when you pick up the club for the first time next season. Notice how natural and unforced the swing feels after the winter off. Sure, your overall game will be a bit rusty, but your swing may follow its groove better than ever!

CHAPTER THREE

Grooving a Great Swing

3

We are what we repeatedly do. Excellence, then, is not an act, but a habit. —Aristotle

The search for the perfect swing is a lifelong endeavor for many golfers. Such a holy-grail-type search undoubtedly becomes a source of great frustration, and leads to constant swing experimentation and a decided lack of perfection. Sadly, the goal of acquiring a perfect-looking Tiger-like swing is illogical and a waste of precious time. Since we all possess unique physiques, we all have a different "perfect swing." Your goal is to develop the most effective swing given your genetics and body build, one that produces consistent, predictable results. It may not be picture perfect, but neither are those of Arnold Palmer, Jim Furyk, and a host of other winners I could list.

With this in mind, this chapter presents the swing fundamentals on which to build an effective swing according to your physiology. If you possess a swing that produces consistent, predictable results, then you can move on to the next chapter. If you lack confidence in your swing, however, I encourage you to work through the drills in this chapter, despite their basic nature. Perform them regularly for a few months, and at the same time build them into your play. With this strategy, you can reengineer your swing and increase its effectiveness at long last. Of course, I strongly encourage you to seek professional one-on-one instruction to supplement the techniques and strategies covered in this book.

If you are an experienced golfer currently struggling with your swing, please proceed to "Error Detection and Correction" beginning on page 59. Here you will find the tips for correcting most ball-flight problems. I also recommend you begin using some of the drills detailed in this chapter.

For beginners, this chapter is your focal point for the coming weeks. Let me emphasize that grooving a good swing is your primary mission—that means developing a smooth, effective swing that is second nature and always identically repeatable. During your first few weeks and months in the sport, your mind will be brimming with swing thoughts and your swing will be evolving each day. Relax and enjoy the process of learning the swing despite the inevitable difficulties—this is a vital distinction, because stress and overexpectancy will develop a habit of tension and anxiety that will plague your golf game for years to come.

The long-term goal, of course, is to develop a fundamentally sound setup that can give birth to a consistent golf swing. While this level of perfection can take years to develop, a logical progression of smart practice can speed up the process of grooving a good swing. This allows you to progress to training other aspects of the game sooner, because you've built a sound foundation. Thus it's critical not to put the cart before the horse by moving on to the more difficult clubs and skills before you've acquired a reasonable level of success at the basic swing. This is one of the most common errors among golfers, leading to the lifelong frustration of an ever-changing swing that never grooves. As a passionate junior golfer always wanting to learn more, I was reminded many times by my father to be "patient, patient, patient." "In time," he'd say, "you'll groove a great swing!"

Developing a Good Setup

As mentioned in chapter 1, the golf swing is a chain reaction event beginning from the setup. A bad setup all but guarantees a bad swing and shot, whereas a good setup means you at least have a chance at a good swing and outcome. With beginners, I spend much of the first lesson or two working the setup and basic swing mechanics, hardly ever hitting a ball. In the earliest stages of learning it's especially important to focus on the process (the swing) while ignoring the outcome (the ball flight). Thus, it is best to resist the natural tendency of wanting to swing at a ball every time and instead spend a lot of time working on your setup and swing without the pressure of having to make ball contact (often a hard thing for a true novice).

Also, I believe it's easiest to learn the golf swing if you practice exclusively with a single club for the first couple of weeks. This eliminates having to worry about the slight repositioning of your body and changing ball position required when hitting different clubs. It also tightly blocks the practice swings you'll be taking, meaning that you'll groove the correct feel and motor skills more quickly and accurately. I encourage you to carry only your 7-iron to the practice range, leaving the rest of your clubs at home so as not to tempt you. Certainly this one-club philosophy can be frustrating if you've just fallen in love with the game (or bought a brand-new set of clubs). Trust me, though: Breaking out the other clubs too early is a mistake you'll pay for in terms of ongoing frustration as the struggle to find your swing continues on and on.

A good starting position is important in all sports, but especially in swing sports such as golf. When in the correct setup position, your body can more easily execute the desired motion in a natural way. It may not feel natural at first, but most sports skills don't the first time around. (Remember how hard riding a bike or skiing felt the first time?) Time invested in getting it right from the start will save you a lifelong struggle of constantly changing your setup in the hope of finding a more comfortable and effective starting position. Acute attention to the details of the setup and swing help you understand the mechanics involved and, thus, increase the odds that you'll successfully learn the skill. Sans-ball swing practice, to start, heightens this awareness and will maximize your learning.

The three aspects of the setup are grip, posture, and alignment. All are equally important and all have a small range of correct positioning. My photographs show the normal textbook positions for each aspect, but remember that your unique physique may require a slight modification of this perspective. If you do modify your setup from these ideal positions, err on the side of too little change, as opposed to great variation from the norm. If at all in doubt about the correctness of your setup, please see a teaching professional before you start down the road of incorrect learning—a road that is far more difficult to reverse with every passing practice and season.

The Grip

There are three different grips used for taking full-swing shots: the overlapping, the interlocking, and the two-handed "baseball" grip. While the latter grip may feel more comfortable to a novice, I recommend that only children and petite women (who tend to have smaller hands) experiment with it. Otherwise, I advise you to try both the interlocking and overlapping during your initial lesson or two, and settle in quickly with the one that feels most right and secure to you. Some people find the interlocking more secure, which they feel allows for a more relaxed grip and better feel. I've always used the traditional overlapping, simply because it's what I was taught and it still works for me.

For the right-handed golfer, the left hand goes on the club first. (If you're left-handed, of course the following instructions should be reversed.) Begin with your left hand slightly cupped. Position the last few inches of the club grip so the grip runs diagonally from the middle joint of your index finger, to the middle joint of the middle finger, and then across your cupped palm toward the fleshy part of your hand

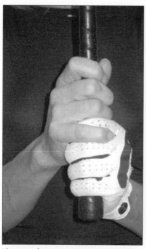

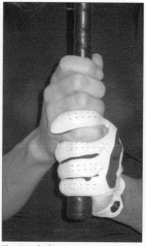

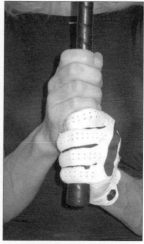

The **overlapping grip,** in which the pinkie finger hooks around the middle knuckle of the index finger.

The **interlocking grip,** in which the pinkie and index finger are interlaced.

The **"baseball" grip,** in which all ten fingers are on the club.

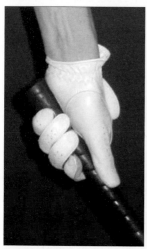

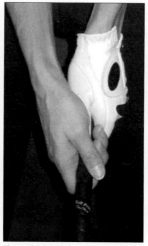

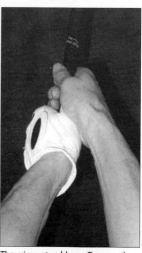

The club handle runs from the heel pad of the palm to the middle joint of the index finger. The thumb extends down the handle. Feel the grip on the club with your last three fingers.

The right hand faces the left hand with the thumb angling left to just touch the index finger. Feel the grip mostly with your middle two fingers.

The view at address: Two or three knuckles of the left hand are visible and the right-hand notch points to the right shoulder. Your overall grip should feel firm, but your forearms should not be tense.

opposite your thumb side. The butt of the club handle should press into this fleshy area, providing enough support so you can hold the club steady by only wrapping your index finger around it. Of course, for the golf swing you'll want all your fingers securely around the handle; in fact, you should feel the grip of the club more in your fingers than in your palm. Finally, your thumb is placed longways down the handle pointing toward the clubhead. Many clubs provide a line or arrow along which to properly align your thumb and grip, although your thumb may actually lie slightly right of this line if your swing requires a stronger grip.

The importance of a correct left-hand setup cannot be overstated, because it's the left hand that gets the clubface square at impact. In comparison, it's best to think of the right hand as merely going along for the ride. With the overlapping grip, begin by placing the right pinkie into the groove between the index and middle fingers of the left hand. Now lightly wrap the rest of your right fingers around the club handle, allowing the right thumb to meet the right forefinger. The right hand of the interlocking and two-handed grips differs from the overlapping grip only in the positioning of the pinkie before you wrap the rest of your fingers. With the interlocking grip, the right pinkie goes between the left index and middle fingers and locks over the back-of-hand first knuckle. The two-handed grip is as simple as wrapping the fingers of your right and left hands around the handle, with the right pinkie butted up against (but not over the top of) the index finger of the left hand. This is similar to the way you grip a baseball bat, although the golf club should sit more in your curled fingers and not in the palm as a bat would.

The final check of your grip involves both kinesthetic and visual acuity. In time, these checks will become second nature, but early on they must be included as part of your setup ritual. First, consider the tightness of your grip. It should be firm, yet relaxed and sensitive enough to allow a good feel of the clubhead. Check this by doing a little waggle or slight swinging of the clubhead. Second, confirm the correct alignment of the grip by examining the notch formed by the thumb and index finger of each hand. The notch formed by the right hand should point toward the right shoulder, while the left-hand notch points more toward your left collarbone (though this will vary depending on how strong a grip you use). These are not absolute positions, however; your unique body build may require slight variations. Consult a teaching professional to verify that your grip is ideal for your physiology.

Posture

Assume a stance with your feet slightly wider than your shoulders, so that when you look down your shoulders appear to fit into the space between your feet. Such a broad stance (and spiked shoes) provides a solid foundation over which you can transfer weight and multiply the power of your swing. Bend slightly at the hips and at the same time allow your rear end to shift slightly backward, as in the very beginning of a sit-down motion. This bent-over position fosters a natural hang of your arms straight down from your shoulders to the ground.

Now you can comfortably take your grip on the club and dangle your arms naturally in front of your body. The left arm should be straight and firm, but not stiff and tense, while the right arm should be relaxed with the elbow hanging near your right hip. Proper posture and arm hang will place the club-handle cap about a hand width (with fingers spread) from the inside of your left thigh. You can easily check this distance by removing your right hand from the club and measuring the space with your outspread hand.

Set up with your feet about shoulder width apart. Your weight should be evenly distributed, but feel the weight more on the insteps of your feet. The left arm is straight and firm, while the right is relaxed and slightly bent. This will set your right shoulder lower than the left.

Bend from the hips and allow your arms to dangle naturally (feel gravity's pull). The spine angle should be nearly straight from the hips to the shoulders, and remain this way through the swing. Check that the club-handle cap is about one hand width from the inside of your left thigh.

Alignment

Golf is a target-oriented sport, making proper alignment as critical as the swing itself. Obviously, a great swing and perfect ball flight will produce poor results on the course if your alignment is off. Too many golfers simply guess at alignment, preferring to focus on the details of the swing itself. Since you want to excel in golf, however, you must dedicate a definite portion of your preshot ritual to focusing solely on alignment (see the sample preshot routine on page 49). Every shot you take, whether at practice or play, should be "locked on target" with the alignment method below.

Since your perspective of alignment is skewed while standing over the ball, you must always start the alignment process from behind the ball. Here you can easily visualize a straight line from the ball to the target (or desired landing spot). Once you "see" this line, scan back from the target to the ball and identify a spot on the line a few feet in front of the ball. This spot is important to guide your alignment as you stand over the ball. It must be specific and small in size. For example, pick an object such as a small leaf, twig, tuft of grass, or divot, and the target line will be obvious and easy to see from over the ball. Otherwise you'll need to imagine a targeting spot in the grass and be careful to keep your eye on it as you walk over to address the ball.

Square your feet, hips, and shoulders to the target line. Visualize this body line and the target line as forming railroad tracks to the target—it can help to place two clubs on the ground to reveal these "tracks."

Begin your address by placing the clubface behind the ball and square to the target line you've envisioned running from the ball to your targeting spot. Now take your grip, and then assume a stance over the ball (for a 7-iron, the ball position is in the middle) with your feet, hips, and shoulders—your body line—parallel to the imaginary target line. Visualize the body and target lines running toward the target like railroad tracks. Now assume proper posture and double-check that the clubface remains square. During early practice sessions, it may help to lay a spare club just in front of your toes and parallel to the target line, so that you can more easily align your shoulders and hips along the body line.

Preshot Routine

To a novice, the many details of grip, posture, and alignment can be overwhelming and hard to remember. Having a detailed preshot routine will help you get it right every time. This way you'll develop good habits and maximize the quality of your setup and swing. Here are the mandatory parts of the preshot routine:

1. Walk behind the ball and pick a target alignment spot a few feet in front of it.

2. Address the ball by first placing your club behind the ball and square to the target line.

3. Take your grip before finalizing your stance—this helps place you at the correct distance from the ball

4. Set your stance with feet slightly wider than shoulder width and be sure your feet, hips, and shoulders are parallel to the target line.

5. Check to see that the ball is in the correct position (the middle of the stance for the 7-iron) and then double-check that your clubface is still square to the target line.

6. Take a slow, tension-releasing breath and relax! You may also find that a small waggle helps control tension and creates a rhythm for initiating your swing.

Learning the Swing with a 7-Iron

Knowledge of the mechanics and muscles used in a golf swing will enhance your learning and lead to long-term excellence. Accordingly, my teaching methods include elements of physiology and physics. Possessing this knowledge not only aids in the initial stages of learning the swing, but also empowers you to detect swing errors based on what you feel during the swing and observe during ball flight (more on this in a bit).

First, you must realize that your shoulders, torso, and legs possess the strongest muscles in your body. It is here where much of the energy that powers the golf swing is derived; in fact, maximum distance and consistency cannot come without proper involvement of these body parts. I point this out because it's quite natural for a beginner to overfocus on what the hands and arms are doing, and thus foster fundamental errors in these other areas.

Golf is, for right-handers, a left-sided sport (and I will continue to use this perspective, since it's most common). The left hand initiates the swing and controls the clubface throughout the swing, whereas the right hand is more of a passive partner along for the ride. It's important to recognize that the right hand itself contributes very little to defining the swing motion, and, thus, many swing errors originate when the right hand becomes too active. Interestingly, this is a very natural tendency since right-handers use their strong right hand for most other sport actions (throwing a baseball, for instance, or swinging a tennis racquet).

The Backswing

From the setup position, consider the V formed by your arms and hands as a unit that moves together. The left arm should remain nearly straight through the complete backswing. At the same time, the right arm bends at the elbow to maintain the same size and shape of the V during the course of the backswing.

Begin the backswing with the left hand pushing the club straight back along the ground, but move the V back together as a unit. Almost immediately the left shoulder begins to follow, and the clubhead will begin its move inside as the club goes farther back. Keep your eyes fixed on the ball and your head relatively still as the left shoulder continues to turn, toward a position under your chin. Meanwhile, your torso and hips begin to rotate as your weight shifts increasingly onto the right instep. Your left wrist cocks toward the end of this turn, as your left shoulder approaches the "down" position. At the top of the backswing you should feel more weight on the instep of the right foot than on your left foot—the heel of which may or may not come off the ground—but you should still feel balanced and stable.

As a warning, don't force too much shoulder and torso rotation; it requires significant flexibility to complete a pro-like turn with the shoulders in a vertical position. Many golfers force this turn and end up lifting their left heel too much or even shifting or swaying their body away from the ball—and both actions destroy the swing. Regular practice combined with daily stretching (see chapter 7) will gradually increase your ability to complete the turn.

The Downswing

Whereas the backswing stores energy like a compressed spring, the downswing releases the energy in a process that multiplies the force as it translates to the clubface at impact. The resulting explosion jettisons the ball farther than in any other swing sport—as much as a quarter mile in the case of an extreme drive.

The downswing begins with a lower-body weight shift to the left. This allows you to pull with your left arm and begin the uncoiling of your torso. Your wrists remain cocked as your legs drive laterally toward the target. As the weight shift nears completion, the wrists release and the hands and arms become square at impact, exactly as they were positioned behind the ball during the setup. Maximum clubhead speed occurs at this time, and the release funnels energy to the end of the club in a whiplike fashion.

Swing Sequence—Irons

1

Set up with the ball midstance (7-iron). The left arm is straight and firm, while the right is relaxed and slightly bent. Notice that the arms and hands form a large V pointing toward the ball.

2

The backswing begins with the left hand starting the V straight back together as a unit. The shoulders, however, produce most of the movement as the torso begins to coil.

5

The downswing begins with a lower-body weight shift to the left. The torso begins to uncoil—first at the hips, followed by the shoulders. Hands remain cocked as the legs drive laterally toward the target.

6

As the weight shift nears completion, the hands release into the impact zone, allowing the clubhead to become square at impact. Notice that the head stays down through impact.

3

The left shoulder continues to turn down as the club-head moves inside. Weight shifts increasingly onto the right instep as the hips follow the turn. The eyes remain fixed on the ball with the head relatively still.

4

The top position, with the hands cocked and the left shoulder under the chin. Notice the club is nearly parallel to the ground and the left arm is reasonably straight, but not forced to be rigid.

7

The arms rotate as they follow the rotation of the body. Naturally, the head begins to lift and turn toward the target.

8

Weight goes fully onto the left side as the body extends and the hands and arms naturally follow through to the classic finish.

At the top of the backswing, the left arm is nearly straight, the right elbow is positioned down toward the hip, and the V formed by the forearms remains intact. From here, the club can swing down inside and release straight down the target line.

At the finish, weight is shifted almost completely onto the left foot, the torso faces the target, and the hands come to rest over the left shoulder and behind the left ear. The finish is relaxed and stable—hold it for a couple of seconds as if posing for a picture.

The Follow-Through

Through impact, the arms rotate as they follow the rotation of your body. Finally, your head can begin to turn toward the target. Hands and arms follow through high, as your shoulders and your hips end up facing the target. Ideally, the swing ends in the classic finish position with nearly all your weight on the left foot and only the toe of your right shoe touching the ground.

Swing Cues

Relax and allow arms to hang naturally, swing easy and smooth, lead the club back and through with the left hand, right hand only along for the ride, coil and uncoil torso, follow-through high and balanced.

Practicing the Swing

If you are a beginner, start each practice session with ten to twenty swings without a ball. As stated earlier, it's much easier to begin grooving golf's motor skills without the stress and pressure of having to hit a ball. Still, visualize a target, target line, and body line so you have a reference with which to square your body during setup and a target to release toward. Take your time with these practice swings and be religious in their use; they're critical for developing proper muscle memory, feel, and confidence. Patience during this a stage of learning will in the future pay off many times over as you move on to learning other clubs with a stable, confident swing.

Next, repeat the above process, not yet with the ball, but with the addition of a tee pressed in the ground at the desired ball location (the middle of the stance with the 7-iron). This time you want to concentrate more on the tee and less on the feel of your body and mechanics of the swing. Begin to let the swing happen. Take ten to twenty practice swings at the tee.

Now you're going to repeat this process and just let the golf ball get in the way! After each shot, hold the finish position for five seconds to develop balance. Beginners should always use a tee—just tee the ball up slightly—and practice with a single club. As discussed in chapter 2, you want to block your practice so each trial is identical. The idea is to groove in the basic swing without the "noise" and confusion of changing conditions and clubs. After a few practice sessions, you can eliminate the tee and begin hitting off a mat or from good lies on the grass.

Initial practice sessions should be of limited length so as not to produce great physical or mental fatigue. It's impossible to learn new skills in a fatigued state; in fact, you are more likely to groove in bad habits if you go overboard on practice early on. Plan on three or four, half- to one-hour sessions per week to start. If you follow the sans-ball practice plan above, you may only have time to hit thirty or so balls during your initial practice sessions.

You can enhance your swing training through use of some targeted practice drills (see "Seven Drills for Grooving a Great Swing"). Perform these drills at the range, before course play, in your backyard, or indoors as winter swing training. Beginners should use these drills a few days per week to accelerate learning of proper mechanics and feel. More advanced players can employ them as part of a pre-practice warm-up routine or as sport-specific strength training via the addition of a swing weight to the club (see chapter 6).

Seven Drills for Grooving a Great Swing

1. Torso Turn Warm-Up Drill

Place a club behind your back running through the bend in each elbow. Assume a standard swing setup and execute the torso rotation just as in a regular swing. Focus on rotating as much as possible through the swing motion without losing balance. Repeat five to ten times.

2. Swoosh Drill

Perform this drill with a long iron or wood, but grab hold of the clubhead with your left hand and extend the grip end down toward the ground. Take a standard stance and perform a one-arm swing, striving to accelerate through the imaginary ball position. When done correctly, you'll hear a *swoosh* only as the club hand accelerates past the impact zone, not during the backswing or the beginning of the downswing. Repeat this swing motion five to ten times.

3. Post-Impact Extension Drill

Begin with both arms straight and the club pointing to the imaginary target, head down over imaginary ball position, and with your right side and right leg released slightly with your heel off the ground. Hold this extended position for three seconds, take a full backswing, and swing through to the finish. Repeat five to ten times back to back without stopping—a good workout!

4. Weight-Shift Swing Drill

Beginning with your feet together, swing the club back, then step with your left foot toward the imaginary target and swing through to the finish. Repeat five to ten times, always beginning each rep with your feet together.

5. One-and-a-Half-Arm Drill

This drill will strengthen your left side—especially the left arm and forearm—as well as help put the clubface in the correct position when you hit the ball. Assume your regular setup, except with your right hand gripping your left wrist. Swing back and hold for one second, then swing through to the finish. Repeat five to ten times.

6. Preset Turning Drill

From a standard setup position, cock your wrists until the club is parallel to the ground. Check to be sure the back-of-hand plane of the left hand is "one" with the back of the wrist–forearm plane, and your right elbow is in toward your hip. Now maintain this arm and hand position as you turn your shoulders back and coil your torso. Begin the down-swing with a lower-body weight shift left, maintaining the wrist cock as long as possible before centrifugal force releases at impact. Finish the swing as usual and hold the classic finish. Repeat five to ten times.

7. Feet-Together Drill

Stand with your feet together (or only a few inches apart) and take five to ten smooth, balanced swings through an imaginary ball position. The narrow stance will reduce the size of your swing and foster better balance, while also fostering better torso rotation and arm swing. Performed regularly, this drill will eliminate lower-body sway while increasing upper-body flexibility and power.

As your shot quality and consistency increase over the first few weeks, you can cease the no-ball practice swings and begin adding some of the drills detailed below. Still, I feel it's better to keep practicing with just one or two clubs during the initial weeks and months of practice.

Error Detection and Correction

As Principle 11 points out, "Professional golf instruction is the optimal method of instruction." A golf professional is also the swing doctor you need to accurately detect and correct swing errors. Still, a pro might not always be around in your time of need, and I'm a firm believer that every golfer should possess a basic understanding of swing mechanics and ball-flight laws.

While the information below is but the tip of the swing-error iceberg, it will enable you to understand and, I hope, correct some gross errors that may occur as your swing develops. The earlier error is detected and corrected, the less it will be grooved into your nervous system, and the less likely it is to resurface sometime in the future. Take a proactive role in fixing your swing, and never put it off until next week or next season. Regular practice or play with a fundamentally flawed swing decreases the chances you'll ever acquire a good swing. Remember, every bad swing you take further hardwires the error.

Ball-Flight Laws

The five laws of ball flight involve the clubhead's speed, path, face position, angle of attack, and location of contact with the ball.

1. **Speed.** Clubhead speed is one of the main factors influencing the distance of ball flight. All other things being equal, a higher clubhead speed means longer ball flight.

2. **Path.** The path of the club at impact is a primary factor in determining the direction of ball flight. For example, an inside-out path through the impact zone will "push" the ball right, whereas an outside-in path will "pull" the ball left of the target.

3. **Face position.** Equally important in determining the direction of ball flight is the position of the clubface at impact. An open clubface means the heel of the clubhead arrives at the ball first, thus imparting a sideways spin and resulting in a slice. Conversely, a closed clubface results in a hook spin.

#3 Face Positions

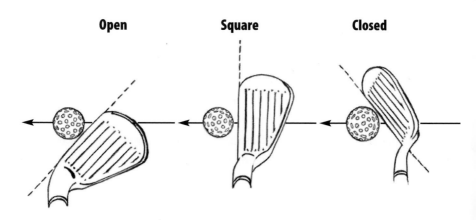

Open　　　　　Square　　　　　Closed

4. **Angle of attack.** The angle of attack involves both the location of contact on the ball and the arc the clubhead is traveling at impact. These factors affect both the distance and the trajectory of the ball flight. Clubface impact above the equator of the ball (topping the ball) results in low flight, or even a roll in extreme

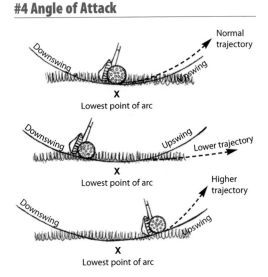

#4 Angle of Attack

cases. Striking the ball below the equator will fly the ball higher. Now consider the arc the clubhead travels and at what point in this arc impact occurs. Normally you'd strike the ball at the bottom of the arc, resulting in normal ball flight. Striking the ball on the downward portion of the arc, however, results in a lower-than-normal shot. As you might expect, impact at the upward part of the arcing clubhead path means a high shot.

5. **Location of contact on clubface.** Where the ball contacts the clubface affects both the distance and the direction of your shot. The ideal is perfect center-face contact on the sweet spot—this yields maximum distance and trueness. The farther the ball is from this sweet spot at contact, the lamer the shot. A shank occurs when ball contact is near the hosel or neck of the club.

Recognizing Gross Errors

Determining a gross error is simply a matter of observing the most common direction and path of ball flight. For instance, consider ten consecutive shots with your 7-iron. While a complete novice may simply spray the balls in a variety of directions, most people settle in on a more common ball flight (swing error). First consider your ball flight. Is it low or high? Then consider the direction of flight. Does it push, slice, pull, or hook? Finally, don't ignore the grossest of gross errors—whiffs and shanks!

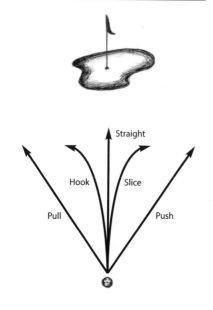

Always begin by examining your setup. I've said this before, but it's worth repeating: A bad setup can doom your swing from the start. It's a common error among high-handicap golfers. Check your grip, body position, and alignment, because all will affect the quality of your shot. If these all check out, however, proceed to the table below for a first guess at your swing error.

Gross Error: Slice (ball curves sharply right of the target line)

Problem 1: Grip too weak (right hand is too far over on top and/or left hand is too far left).

Correction: Reposition your left hand on the club handle so that you can see two or three knuckles. Now place your right hand on the club with the palm facing and flat to the left palm.

Problem 2: Incorrect body alignment (open stance with feet and shoulders aiming left of target).

Correction: Square your shoulders, hips, and feet to the target line. As an aid, place one club along the ball-to-target line and a second club running from toe to toe. The two clubs should be parallel. Practice your preshot routine to foster consistent, proper alignment.

Problem 3: Standing too close to ball (unable to make proper torso rotation on backswing).

Correction: Make sure your arms hang down naturally from your shoulders. Flex slightly at the knees and sit back with your butt slightly out. Now measure for one hand width of distance (use your right hand, with fingers spread out) from the end of the club handle to the inside of your left thigh. Adjust your distance from the ball to allow this ideal distance.

Problem 4: Clubface open at address.
Correction: Focus on clubface alignment when you address the ball. Examine the blade and grooves and make sure they are perfectly perpendicular to the target line before taking your final grip on the club.

Problem 5: Right shoulder too strong (too high and/or too tight).
Correction: Allow your right shoulder to relax and position it slightly lower than the left shoulder. Be careful, however, not to lean to the right (a common overcorrection).

Problem 6: Not following through correctly, so that clubface opens at impact.
Correction: Focus on the feel of the release as the hands and forearms roll through impact. Perform the Feet-Together Drill (see page 59).

Problem 7: Bad balance and poor transfer of weight through to left side.
Correction: Perform the Weight-Shift Swing Drill and the Post-Impact Extension Drill (see page 57).

Gross Error: Push (straight ball flight to the right of target)

Problem 1: Closed stance (the feet or shoulders pointing right of target).
Correction: Place a spare club on the ground running parallel to the target line. Take your stance along this club and align your feet, hips, and shoulders so they are square.

Problem 2: Too much right arm in swing, and poor release.
Correction: Perform the Feet-Together Drill to enhance the feel of left-hand dominance and the correct motion of releasing the hands and forearms through impact. The One-and-a-Half-Arm Drill will also produce the feeling of left-hand dominance that you are after.

Problem 3: Moving your head or swaying toward target.
Correction: Renew your focus on the ball and strive to keep your head steady through impact. Perform the Feet-Together Drill to learn torso turn, balance, and steadiness.

Gross Error: Pull (straight flight left of target due)

Problem 1: Open alignment of the feet, hips, and/or shoulders.

Correction: Relax your right side and carefully square your feet, hips, and shoulders parallel to the target line.

Problem 2: Right-hand grip too strong (too far turned to right).

Correction: Adjust the right-hand grip on the club by turning it slightly counterclockwise until the notch formed by the index finger and thumb points toward your right shoulder.

Gross Error: Hook (ball curves sharply left of the target line)

Problem 1: Grip too strong.

Correction: Regrip by turning your left hand counterclockwise until you can only see one or two knuckles. The notch formed by the left index finger and thumb should point toward your left collarbone, while your right palm should be flat and facing the left palm.

Problem 2: Clubface closed at impact.

Correction: At address, begin by positioning the clubface square to the target line, then proceed to take your left- and right-hand grip on the club. Be sure the clubface remains square after you've taken your grip and stance.

Problem 3: Aligned to right of target.

Correction: Set your body line parallel to the target tine. Lay two clubs on the ground, one along the target line and the other along the body line, to help you visualize the "railroad tracks" to the hole.

Problem 4: Improper hand cock with left wrist flex.

Correction: Perform the Preset Turning Drill to learn proper cock position. The left wrist should be in a neutral position—the same plane as your forearm.

Gross Error: Low ball flight due to topping the ball

Problem 1:   Tension at setup.

Correction: Perform the ANSWER Sequence described in chapter 6 prior to address. Consider adding a waggle or slight swinging of the club during your setup in order to prevent tension buildup.

Problem 2:   Setup too far from ball.

Correction: Measure for correct distance at setup by using your right hand to check the distance from the club-handle cap to the inside of your left thigh. The width of your spread-out hand (pinkie to thumb) should just fit in this space.

Problem 3:   Too much use of right side in swing motion.

Correction: Relax your right side and focus on allowing the left hand to take the club back through the backswing and then lead the club to the ball on the downswing. Perform the One-and-a-Half-Arm Drill.

Problem 4:   Standing too tall or hesitancy to hit down on the ball and take a divot.

Correction: Without a ball, practice swinging down through a golf tee pressed almost all the way down into the grass. Focus on taking a smooth swing and attempt to break the tee as you accelerate through the impact zone. Also, perform the Feet-Together Drill.

Problem 5:   Bent left arm and/or lack of extension at impact.

Correction: Firm up your left arm as if it were in a cast, and maintain this firm feeling during the backswing. Perform the One-and-a-Half-Arm Drill. (Note: Lack of flexibility and strength makes keeping a straight left arm difficult for some people. Don't get overly concerned, because a slight bend on the backswing will usually straighten out on the downswing.)

Problem 6:   Poor weight shift or finishing back on right foot.

Correction: Practice with a three-quarter swing and exaggerated lower-body movement. Focus on initiating the downswing with a lower-body weight shift. Hold the finish for three seconds after each shot. Also, perform the Weight-Shift Drill.

CHAPTER FOUR

Learning Your Irons and Woods

4

Life affords no higher pleasure than that of surmounting difficulties, passing from one step of success to another, forming new wishes and seeing them gratified. —Samuel Johnson

This chapter is about learning to make solid clubhead-to-ball contact with the rest of the clubs in your bag with minimal anguish and without unlearning or polluting the good swing you developed in the previous chapter. Of course, if you haven't yet acquired a decent swing with your 7-iron (a reasonable level of success is 50 percent straight, sound shots), you'll only exacerbate your struggle and frustrations by progressing to the other clubs too soon. Certainly a bag full of new clubs is tantalizing, but breaking them out too early may hamper your swing training and could result in you never perfecting the very clubs you want so much to learn.

Early learning of golf skills is a step-by-step process. The initial focus on learning the fundamentals of a good swing with a single club eventually graduates to a one-by-one addition of new clubs to your repertoire. Take this approach and you'll come a long way in your first season or two in this sport, breaking 100, then 90, then 85 before you know it. Conversely, impatience and succumbing to the natural desire to grip and rip with every club in your bag will leave you living in the rough and woods and maybe, in time, at the Betty Ford clinic!

With this in mind, let me emphasize that a group of beginning golfers with equal patience and desire will each progress at a different rate, performance-wise. Despite an identical approach to their golf training, other factors such as available time, general physical conditioning, and natural hand–eye coordination allow some people to advance faster than others. For this reason, I don't present a firm time line for introducing new skills and practice techniques. The most basic stage of learning described in the previous chapter could take a week, a month, or a year to achieve. Likewise, some golfers will be able to acquire many of the skills in this chapter in a single season, while for others it could take years. By following the strategies I present, you ensure high practice efficacy (the power to be productive) and the fastest rate of progress given your available time and natural skill.

Learning the 6- and 8-Irons

If you've achieved an 50 percent success rate with the 7-iron, you'll make short work of learning the 6- and 8-iron. These clubs vary by only about half an inch in length from your 7-iron and feel only slightly different. In fact, learning these new clubs may be more of a mental than a physical challenge—many people get psyched out just knowing there's a different number club in their hands. I've noticed that if I sneak a 6- or 8-iron into the hands of a student who thinks he's still hitting with a 7-iron, he'll hit some great shots immediately. The pressure of acquiring a new skill was removed—he thought he was swinging his 7-iron!

You may not be able to trick yourself in quite this way, but you can get a similar effect during your initial practice with the 6- and 8-iron by visualizing that you're still hitting with the 7-iron. After hitting twenty or thirty shots with your 7-iron, casually swap in your 6-iron and just keep on hitting. Don't make an event of it; in fact, change nothing. The ball position is the same (the middle of the stance), and your setup and swing should not be much different. Take twenty or thirty shots, then go back and hit another ten with your 7-iron.

As in learning any new skill, the initial practice sessions must be blocked in nature. Hit from perfect lies and toward the same target. Concern yourself only with swinging smoothly and making solid ball contact, and, for now, forget about how far your shots travel. If you focus on the fact that your 6-iron shots should go farther than those with your 7-iron, you'll naturally overswing. This is one of the more common problems I see with golfers struggling to learn a new club, so you must acknowledge this and resist it. Trying to make the extra yardage happen will degrade your swing and ensure the opposite. Be patient, be confident, and let it happen. In time you'll find you're getting roughly ten yards more carry thanks to effective use of your tool, and not as a result of swinging harder.

Use the same method for adding the 8-iron to your arsenal. If you felt comfortable with your 6-iron shots, you might try twenty or thirty shots with your 8-iron during the same practice session. Otherwise, acknowledge that you're tired and that little or no motor learning can occur, and save your 8-iron until the next practice session. As in learning the 6-iron, relax and do everything the same as you did when hitting with your 7-iron. Feel confident in this similarity, and let the swing happen.

Eight-iron shots typically travel about ten yards less than 7-iron, and the ball flight will be slightly higher. Again, I urge you to focus on a quality swing and let the distances happen. Over the course of many weeks and months of practice, you'll develop a good sense of distance for each club.

Spend a minimum of two to three weeks practicing your 6-, 7-, and 8-irons before moving on to other clubs. During this time, progress from blocked to variable practice as your skills improve. As explained in chapter 2, you need to develop motor learning schemas in your nervous system over the range of conditions that you may encounter on the course. This is easily done at a natural-grass driving range by varying the lie of the ball. Place the ball in a variety of less-than-perfect lies, such as in thicker or thinner spots in the grass or in locations where the ground seems harder or softer than normal. Take twenty to thirty shots each with the 6-, 7-, and 8-irons.

Initially your percentage of nice shots will decrease because you're practicing under conditions far different from the perfectly blocked practice to which you are accustomed. That's good; in fact, that's golf! Relax, and accept the bad shots as part of the learning process (remember, you left your ego at home). In time, your nervous system will develop detailed code enabling you to hit great shots from a wide variety of lies.

Next you need to learn to hit these great shots with the first swing of the club, not only after ten, twenty, or thirty tries. Random practice is the ticket here. If your frequency of good, clean shots with your 6-, 7-, and 8-irons is around 50 percent, you're ready. Don't rush into this third step in learning—it could take anywhere from just a few sessions to as long as a season for some people to progress this far. As mentioned at the outset of this chapter, I think rushing to learn new clubs and advanced techniques will multiply your frustrations as well as the time it takes to learn the skills of golf.

Random practice is just what the name says—practice with a random choice of clubs, lies, and targets. This is the most powerful method of driving-range practice, because it's exactly what you have to do at the course. (Sadly, I see few people do anything but blocked practice at the range.) After a warm-up of ten to twenty variable practice shots with each of your three clubs, begin a one-shot-per-club shootout at different targets on the range. Tap one ball at a time from the ball pile and hit from whatever lie it ends up in. Perform your complete preshot routine: Sight the target line from behind the ball, take a practice swing, then address the ball and pull the trigger.

No matter the result of the shot, pick up a different club and align to a different target. This might not seem like effective practice, especially after a horrible shot. But by taking a second shot with the same club, you'd start a habit of wanting to take a second shot after every less-than-ideal shot. This second-chance option becomes a part of your subconscious, leading to less focus on the first shot and poorer performance. The power of random practice is that you learn to perform at a high level the first time—because you have to! Ditto on the golf course. Performance will soar as your motor skills have been conditioned for instant, one-try recall. What's more, focus and confidence will be yours, because you've been trained to make every shot count.

Cues for the 6- and 8-Irons

> Think it's a 7-iron, trust the swing, easy does it on the backswing, stay down and watch for the divot.

Learning the Short Irons: 9-Iron, Pitching Wedge, and Sand Wedge

The short irons are great stroke savers—as long as you possess the confidence in these tools that comes only through many dedicated golf training sessions. The wide variety of skills you'll need to learn include both full- and partial-swing shots. In this chapter I'm going to discuss only the full-swing shots. The numerous and equally important partial-swing shots are covered in the next chapter, however, and they can be learned in the same time frame as this chapter's full-swing skills. I suggest you read this chapter and the next, then begin practice of both full- and partial-swing shots.

Ideal Ball Flight

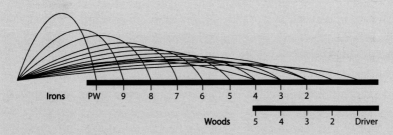

With a full swing, the 9-iron, pitching wedge, and sand wedge produce a high ball flight and significant backspin. The combined effect is little or no roll—perfect for dropping balls on the green and, hopefully, near the pin. Developing a modest level of confidence and accuracy takes the average person anywhere from two weeks to two months of dedicated practice. Proceed slowly and patiently through the three practice methods—blocked practice to begin learning, then variable and random practice as you become more proficient.

Prepare for your short-iron shots with the same preshot routine as for the middle irons. Determine the target line

The short irons require a few modifications at address. Play the ball slightly back of center stance, bend a little more at the hips, and flex a bit more at the knees.

and a start-over spot in front of the ball. At address, you'll need to make a few minor modifications, since these clubs range from one-half to two inches shorter than your middle irons. First, move the ball position right of the midstance position by one to two ball widths. This slight ball shift back in the stance accommodates the shorter clubs.

Your stance also needs to be adjusted for the shorter club length. Bend a bit more at the hips, sit back with your butt, and flex a slight bit more at your knees. Arms still hang naturally from the shoulders to the ground, your grip remains unchanged, and the club-handle cap should still point to the inside of your left thigh. Because of these changes, your view at address will look a little different. Don't be alarmed; it's correct for the setup to look and feel a little different. In fact, these differences are some of the subtleties of the game you need to dial if you are ever to excel.

Look for these subtle differences each time you setup with the short irons. With the ball back in the stance, your hands will look to be farther ahead of the ball than with your middle irons. That's fundamentally correct. Don't change it! Also, since you're sitting down and bent over a bit more, you'll feel closer to the ball. That also is correct. If you think you're too close, however, do the "hand check." Measure the distance between the club handle cap and the inside of your left thigh—it should be about the distance from the pinkie to the thumb of your spread-out right hand.

The swing is basically unchanged, except that it won't be as big as with the middle irons. A controlled, smooth, and balanced swing is paramount with these more delicate tools. I tell my students that the swing should feel like a three-quarter swing compared to the middle irons. Trying to match the swing you perform with your longer irons will produce an overswing and possibly cause you to lift up and top the ball.

I suggest you take a practice swing before each short-iron shot. Set up over the ball and square to the target line, yet far enough away from the ball so you won't hit it during your practice swing. The practice swing helps your nervous system adjust to the shorter length club and learn the feel of swinging through the grass. Therefore, it's vital that you stay down through the practice swing and take a slight divot or cut through the grass. Don't be shy about it—visualize the ball and swing through it, looking for the divot before you turn your head to the target. Now step up to the ball and repeat the same swing through the real ball—remember to use the location of your contact with the grass on the practice swing to more precisely position the ball in your stance.

Solid, center-of-clubface contact with the short irons results in significantly higher ball flight compared to the middle-length clubs. If you don't get that result, you're probably not staying down on the ball and taking enough of a divot. Granted, the ground conditions affect the degree to which you can take a divot. Most golf courses and some driving ranges are watered enough that your club will easily slice through the turf, creating a nice divot (that should be replaced). However, drier ground and, of course, range mats limit your ability to swing down through the ball. Although it is good to occasionally practice under such adverse conditions, they do make learning to take divots difficult.

Cues for the 9-Iron and Wedges

Relax and swing easy, take what feels like a three-quarter swing, pull club-handle cap to the ball, watch for the divot to appear, follow through to balanced finish.

Practicing the 9-Iron

It's best to learn the short irons in descending order of length, so let's begin with the 9-iron. First, take ten or twenty warm-up shots with your middle irons. Once you feel you're swinging well, it's time to begin work on the 9-iron.

The goal is to hit twenty to thirty balls with the 9-iron. Each shot should be preceded by a practice swing through the turf; then step up to the ball and take a nice, easy swing. As in learning any new skill, the practice should be blocked. Give yourself perfect lies and aim at the same target for each shot. In future practice sessions, employ variable and then randomized practice methods as the overall quality of your shots improves.

Strive for a smooth, steady practice session, as you do a smooth, balanced swing. With blocked practice, it's natural to begin rushing your shots since the target and lie are the same each time. Resist this tendency by walking behind the ball before each shot and visualizing the ideal ball flight and landing zone. This process of going through your preshot routine, taking a practice swing, and then taking a real swing at the ball might take thirty seconds or more. All totaled your twenty to thirty warm-up shots and the twenty to thirty practice shots with the 9-iron will take about thirty to forty-five minutes. That's fine, because in swing training it's quality that counts, not quantity.

Swinging the Pitching Wedge

Upon developing a high success rate with your 9-iron, you can move on to the pitching wedge. Use the same basic practice protocol as in learning the 9-iron. Begin with some 7-iron shots until your swing feels smooth and balanced, and then hit ten to twenty balls with your 9-iron. This process primes the nervous system for rapid learning of the next shorter club—the pitching wedge. As before, block your initial twenty or thirty shots. Hitting this club should come easily, with an ideal ball flight slightly higher than your 9-iron and about ten yards shorter. Continue training with blocked practice for as many sessions as it takes to reach 50 percent solid, straight shots.

Over the course of a couple of weeks, confidence and feel with your 9-iron and pitching wedge will increase, as will your knowledge of the average distance each club produces. Remember that it's the average, not maximum, distance of a club that you want to identify for proper club selection on the course. As your swing grooves, overall quality of shots will increase and the average distance will increase toward the maximum.

Learning to Hit the Sand Wedge

Upon picking up the sand wedge, you'll notice that it's surprisingly heavy despite its modest size. The extra weight is in the clubhead, which is specially designed for getting balls out of the sand. But don't let the name fool you; the sand wedge rules equally for making critical fairway shots at the pin.

Unfortunately, this short, highly lofted, and weighty club is the toughest of the three short irons to learn. If you're struggling with hitting your 9-iron and pitching wedge, hold off on adding this club to your practice regimen. In fact, with some students I move on to instruction with the long irons instead of waiting until all the wedges are dialed in.

Whenever you do begin working these shots, they must be blocked and highly repetitive. As a rule, the more difficult a club, the longer you will have to continue with blocked practice. The average golfer probably needs to hit hundreds of quality blocked shots before she develops the level of feel and success needed to move on to the variable and random practice methods. This explains why many golfers seem to struggle forever with a certain club (such as the sand wedge). They simply never hit enough balls or lack the proper setup and swing to begin with! For instance, they hit twenty or thirty perfect shots with their pitching wedge, and figure that just a few shots with the similar sand wedge will be enough. Wrong! If anything, they should be hitting more shots with the sand wedge, because it's the harder club to learn.

Playing for Practice

Playing for practice provides an invaluable combination of experience and motor learning. Ideally, you want to wait until you've logged two to three months of regular practice and learned the basics of chipping and putting (as described in chapter 5) before committing to this adventure. Gauge your readiness for the links by hitting ten shots with a random variety of short and middle irons. If you can classify more than half the shots as good, then you're ready. To wait any longer would not only stunt your learning of the game's many facets, but also keep you from enjoying some good fun on the links.

For the rest of your first season, plan on a once-a-week outing to the local par-3 or pitch-and-putt facility. Forget about trying to play full-length courses for now; the skills required for "survival" can't be learned in a few months. Par-3 courses are ideal because they require only the middle and short irons and your putter. Furthermore, these courses are quite forgiving, with nearly flat lies and only a handful of bunkers. More important, the majority of golfers here are beginners, so the inevitable foul ball or whiff is nothing extraordinary.

Learning to play in such a low-pressure environment is critical. Your first few golf outings largely shape your habits and ability to relax and function on the course in the years to come. If you spend your first season playing fun, low-key par-3s, you'll create positive beliefs and good habits that carry over to full-length course play in the future. Conversely, the high levels of tension and bad habits many experienced golfers perpetually carry with them were programmed during early fiascoes that resulted from trying to play a full-length course too soon.

Learning Your Long Irons: 5-Iron, 4-Iron, and 3-Iron

The long irons are some of the most crucial clubs when playing full-length courses. On many par-4 holes you'll need to carry 150 to 220 yards on your second shot to reach the green in regulation. In these situations, you'll likely use either a 5-, 4-, or 3-iron or your 7-, 5-, or 3-wood (to be discussed next), depending on the distance needed. Unfortunately, the lower the number on the club (longer irons), the more difficult it is to hit. It's not unusual to spend several seasons training to dial in these clubs. But if you've been successful with your short and middle irons, then there's no time like the present to begin learning the longies.

Begin with the 5-iron, and progress to training the 4- and 3-iron as your rate of quality shots reaches about 50 percent with a given club. As in learning the short irons, you'll need to modify the basic setup and swing described in chapter 3. Strive for acute awareness of the differences in setup and feel of the swing with the long irons. You can then make the necessary adjustments to foster the good form and feel each time you pick up a long iron.

At address, position the ball left of center with longer clubs. Ideal ball position for the 3-iron is a few inches left of center. For the 4- and 5-irons, position the ball roughly one to two ball widths left of center. Your stance also needs to be modified to accommodate the longer club shafts. Stand a bit taller with less bend at the waist and only a slight bend in your knees. Let your arms hang freely from the shoulders, with a slight "reach" toward the ball with the longest clubs. Finally, check for balance and even weight distribution on your feet.

Swinging these long clubs definitely feels different from the shorter irons—in particular, the swing timing is much different, which is one reason so many people struggle with these clubs. On the backswing, it should feel like you are dragging the club back along the ground longer before the shoulder turn takes over and lifts the club in the air behind you. Stay relaxed in the hands and feel for the weight of the clubhead and the hand cock. Begin the downswing with the lower body and feel the left side pull down through the ball. This action (and swing thought) helps encourage proper release of the forearms, improves extension, and stores up

With the long irons, it's important to stand taller and position the ball left of center stance. Arms hang naturally, but with a slight reach toward the ball.

more energy for maximum clubhead speed at impact.

It's important that you resist the natural tendency to swing faster and harder with these clubs. The longer shaft and less-lofted clubface produce extra distance without consciously taking a home run swing. In fact, many high-handicap golfers find they get more distance by taking a three-quarter swing instead of a less pure full swing. Less-lofted clubs are more sensitive to gross errors, and since the ball carries farther even small misses result in large deviations from the target line. Employ the Feet-Together Drill (see page 59) to help you develop proper torso turn and a smooth, relaxed swing. Alternate between hitting a few shots with a regular stance and a few with your feet together.

Utilize the same practice strategy for training with the long irons. Blocked practice should reign for as long as it takes to develop feel, confidence, and a reasonable rate of success with a given club. Variable practice then takes over as the power tool for learning these clubs from a variety of lies. It may take some time, but you can eventually add the long irons to your random practice and, of course, your course play.

Cues for the 5-, 4-, and 3-Irons

Begin swinging with a slow drag back, coil and uncoil, steady tempo, accelerate through the ball, and watch for the grass to appear from under the ball.

Learning to Hit the Fairway Woods and Driver

Many golfers find fairway woods easier to hit than the longest of the irons. As a rule, if you swing a 5-iron well, you can begin training with your 7-, 5-, and 3-woods. On the course these clubs are great substitutes for and often better choices than the long irons for second shots on par-4 and par-5 holes. Off the tee

Setup with the woods and driver requires a slightly wider than shoulder width stance. Align the ball position with the left heel.

Stand more erect with increasing club length, by reducing knee and hip flexion. Arms hang nearly straight down, but with a slight reach with the longer clubs.

the 3-wood is often a better choice than the driver for most mid- to high-handicap players.

For starters, here are a few rules to enhance learning of these clubs. Following them doesn't guarantee immediate success, but I've found that many golfers achieve a reasonable rate of success in just a few weeks by abiding by them.

1. Get to work practicing your woods early in your session. Waiting to practice the woods until after hitting through all the irons is a common mistake. Instead hit twenty or thirty warm-up shots with a few of your good clubs, then proceed immediately to practice your focus of the day, in this case the woods. Remember that a fatigued neuromuscular system learns nothing when it comes to acquiring new skills.

2. Hit off a tee during the first few practices with your woods—it's both easier and more forgiving. You'll quickly develop confidence and skill off the tee, at which point you can progress to hitting off the grass. Furthermore, most golfers end up using their 3-wood to tee off for at least their first couple of years in the sport. So it's a club you really need to spend some quality time practicing. Tee the ball at a height that allows the top of the clubhead to strike the ball at its equator. You'll thus need to tee

the ball higher for the larger clubheads of the 3-wood and driver than you would with a 5- or 7-wood.

3. Focus on performing a smooth, controlled, and even-tempo swing. Also, strive to swing smoother, not harder, and let the club do the work. Relax your shoulders and hands, then slowly take the club back, making sure you have good torso rotation and a complete backswing before starting the downswing. Avoid the natural tendency to take a giant swing with your driver. In fact, you may get better results by thinking about taking a three-quarter-sized swing—which in reality may be nearly a correct full-sized swing with your driver. Ironically, I see just the opposite strategy in use at the practice range nearly every day. Trying to do his best John Daly impersonation, a golfer hits a bucket of balls with a big, jerky, and basically out-of-control swing, which produces wildly inconsistent results and surely develops bad swing habits. Don't fall into this trap!

Setup and Swing

Begin by practicing the 5-wood for the first couple of sessions. As you take your stance, position the ball in line with the inside of your left heel. Stand taller than you would with your irons, bending less at the waist and only slightly through the knees. As always, your arms hang naturally from your shoulders, but with a slight reach outward with your hands as you align the clubface behind the ball. When done correctly, this setup positions your left shoulder several inches higher than your right. Now relax through your shoulders and hands, and, if you like, perform a slight waggle as you focus your thoughts for the swing.

Although the swing of a wood is basically the same as an iron, there are a few subtle modifications to help you accommodate the longer, weightier club. I'll describe the swing as it should be executed with a wood.

The backswing begins with your hands, arms, and shoulders moving back together in one piece. Take the clubhead back along the ground for fifteen to twenty inches; you'll feel your arms swing up as your torso rotates. Soon you'll feel the hands cock as they approach a position over your right shoulder. Your left arm should be nearly straight while the right arm is bent at about ninety degrees, with the elbow pointing to the ground. Consider this the top of your backswing—forcing any more of a backswing is unnecessary and will likely cause you problems. Your smooth backswing now gives way to a smooth downswing that begins with a weight shift left in the lower body. Your torso uncoils as your hands lead the clubhead toward the ball. At impact, the clubhead returns to the square position as your forearms and hands release. Your forearms and body continue to turn toward the target as you swing through to a high finish.

Practicing Your 5- and 3-Woods

Hit twenty to thirty balls with your 5-wood, each shot preceded by a practice swing. You can then return to the practice of other skills that you've recently acquired, such as your short irons or chipping and putting. As in learning any new club, focus several practices on learning the new skill. Strive for at least three practice sessions per week, and introduce practice of your 3-wood as soon as your success rate of good 5-wood shots reaches about 50 percent. At this time, you will also want to begin practicing your 5-wood from a variety of grass lies.

There are a couple of very useful drills (see pages 56–59 in chapter 3) to help speed your learning of the woods. The Feet-Together Drill teaches the feel of the hands releasing through impact, while the Weight-Shift Swing Drill focuses on the right-to-left-side weight shift fundamental to swing initiation. The latter exercise is especially helpful if you find yourself hitting the ground behind the ball when swinging your woods.

Cues for the 5- and 3-Woods

Swing within myself, start back low and slow, coil on backswing, keep head steady, left hand leads downswing, sweep the ball off the grass, extend to target.

Practicing Your Driver

High-tech, oversized drivers are the latest rage. Most golfers I meet, even beginners, carry one in their bags. Unfortunately, the driver is one of the last clubs you want to spend time practicing; for many amateurs it's best left in your bag (or at home) when playing on the course.

The problem is this: The driver is the longest and least-lofted club. Getting the clubface consistently square at impact is difficult, and even the slightest mis-alignment or mis-hit is grossly exaggerated. In particular, the cannon shots hit by strong golfers have the opportunity to stray quite far. Meanwhile, weaker golfers often struggle to get the ball up for maximum flight. In either case, hitting a 3-wood off the tee will improve your play.

Swing Sequence—Driver and Woods

Address the ball with the left foot turned slightly outward and the ball aligned to the heel or instep. The right shoulder is set significantly lower than the left, and the large V formed by the arms and hands points toward the ball.

The backswing begins by dragging the club straight back—the V moves back together as a unit. The shoulders immediately begin to turn and the torso begins to coil.

The downswing begins with a lower-body weight shift to the left. The torso begins to uncoil—first at the hips, followed by the shoulders. Hands remain cocked as the legs drive laterally toward the target.

As the weight shift nears completion, the hands release into the impact zone, allowing the clubhead to become square at impact. Notice that the head stays down and behind the ball through impact.

3

The left shoulder continues to turn down as the clubhead moves inside and the hands begin to cock. Weight shifts increasingly onto the right instep as the hips follow the turn.

4

At the top position, hands are cocked and the left shoulder is under the chin. The eyes remain fixed on the ball, but notice that the head is positioned behind the ball. The left arm is neither forced to remain rigid nor allowed to bend at a sharp angle.

7

The arms rotate as they follow the rotation of the body. The head is the last to turn toward the target.

8

Weight goes fully onto the left side as the body straightens and the hands and arms naturally follow through to the classic finish.

At the top of the backswing, the club is parallel to the ground and pointing toward the target. Any more of a backswing *is* overswing!

At the finish, weight is shifted almost completely onto the left foot, the torso faces the target, and the hands come to rest over the left shoulder and behind the left ear.

So when is the right time to begin practice with your driver? When you are consistently hitting your 3-wood straight and long (say, a 50 percent success rate). When you're there, dedicate twenty to thirty balls during the middle part of your practice session to working your driver. Visualize a fairway before each shot. Ideally, your practice range will have a variety of targets, so you can hit between two of them to define the sides of your imaginary fairway.

As your frequency of good shots increases, try it out on some straight and wide holes on your local course. If you can place your drives in the fairway more than 50 percent of the time, then you're ready to incorporate them into your regular play.

Cues for the Driver

Relax grip for soft forearms, low and slow takeaway, make a good turn, shift weight onto left foot to initiate the downswing, left hand leads to the ball, release forearms and body to target, and hold a balanced finish.

Hitting from Uneven Lies

One of the skills you usually can't train at the driving range is hitting from uneven lies. As stressed earlier, playing for practice is invaluable for expanding your command over the irons and woods, and when it comes to uneven lies there's no other way to acquire the skills. While your early visits to flat par-3 courses provide valuable experience and quality random practice, you will have to venture onto more difficult, hilly courses in order to develop skill at hitting from sloping lies.

At first you will find uneven lies stressful and, of course, difficult to hit from effectively. Begin by changing your perspective of these situations—consider them an opportunity, not a curse. Obsessing over score and expecting each shot to be from a perfect lie only increases your stress levels and degrades performance and your ability to learn. As you step up to an uneven-lie shot, then, relax and take a few more extra practice swings than normal. This helps you learn the balance required and primes your neuromuscular system for a shot you may have never before performed. If possible, hit two balls from the problem lie, therefore doubling your practice and increasing skill and confidence.

Volume and frequency of practice are the keys to becoming an expert at such unusual shots. Playing anything less than two or three rounds per month makes learning to hit well from these lies next to impossible. If time and opportunity limit you, purchase a few plastic golf balls and practice on a slope in your backyard or a local park. Assessing the quality of your shots will be difficult, but at least you'll gain experience standing on a slope and swinging the club. Such simulator training can be quite effective in the early stages of learning, but you need to hit real balls in situations that count to progress beyond a beginner's skill level.

There are four basic lies you need to train: uphill (left leg higher), downhill, and sidehill lies with the ball higher and lower than your feet. As you set up in any of these situations, you will naturally find yourself leaning into the hill to straighten your body perpendicular to flat ground. The technique here, however, is to reposition your body perpendicular to the slope, not flat ground. This is achieved in a different way with each type of uneven lie, but the end result is the same— you've "leveled" the lie! You are now in a position to take a mechanically sound swing. But as a rule, you'll need to swing less to maintain balance throughout the swing. Furthermore, you will need to adjust your aim, because each different uneven lie has an inherent effect on ball flight.

Hitting from Uneven Lies

1. Uphill Lie

1. Use a club one size longer than you'd use from this distance with a flat lie, since the ball flight is higher and shorter from an uphill lie. For instance, select a 5-iron instead of a 6-iron.

2. Position the ball slightly forward in your stance—more for steeper hills.

3. Balance your weight more onto the right (downhill) foot.

4. Lower your right shoulder and tilt your torso slightly until the slope of your shoulders roughly parallels the slope of the ground.

5. Take a three-quarter swing and shift your weight into the hill. This helps maintain balance and prevents you from topping the ball (common if too much weight stays on the downhill foot).

2. Downhill Lie

1. Selected a more lofted club (a size shorter) than you'd use from a flat lie at this distance. Avoid using a fairway wood or long iron except on very slight slopes.

2. Position the ball slightly back in your stance—more for steeper hills.

3. Aim slightly left.

4. Balance your weight more onto the left (downhill) foot.

5. Lower your left shoulder and tilt your torso until nearly perpendicular to the slope of the hill.

6. Take a three-quarter swing down the slope.

3. Sidehill with Feet Higher than Ball

1. Position the ball in the middle of a slightly wider-than-normal stance.

2. Aim left of target—more on steeper lies—to compensate for ball flight to right.

3. Stand lower with more bend at the waist and greater knee flex.

4. Find your balance and take a smooth three-quarter swing.

4. Sidehill with Feet Lower than Ball

1. Choke slightly down on the club handle. Choke down lower with increasing height of the ball position above your feet.

2. Position the ball in the middle of the stance.

3. Aim right—more to right with increased severity of slope.

4. Stand taller with less bend at waist and only slight knee flex.

5. Take a controlled swing.

Other Common Shots and Problem Lies

Other common on-course predicaments to prepare for include the inevitable need to hit shots under or over a tree or branch and the occasional deep rough, hardpan, or divot lie. Practice these shots as part of your variable and random practice at the driving range. This way, you'll be confident when faced with such a challenge on the links.

Certainly you'll be dealt your share of trouble shots during your first few years in the sport. But view these situations as opportunities to test the skills you've practiced at the range. Ultimately confidence comes from having been there before, so consider such predicaments as part of the dues-paying and golf training process.

Techniques for Other Problematic Lies

1. Low Shots (under branches or into a strong headwind)

1. Position the ball back in your stance with your hands slightly forward to deloft the clubface.

2. Set your weight more on the left foot and maintain pressure on this foot throughout the swing.

3   Take the club back low and remain low through impact.

2. High Shots (over trees)

1. Position the ball slightly forward in your stance.

2. Move your hands back so the butt of the club faces your crotch (this helps increase loft).

3. Take a normal swing.

3. Deep Rough Lie

1. Select a club based on the length of the rough, not the distance to the target. Deeper rough requires a more-lofted club. Rarely will you be able to hit your longest irons or larger woods out of the rough.

2. Open the clubface slightly and grip the club more firmly with the left hand, since swinging through deep grass tends to close the face.

3. Position the ball midstance with your weight set more on your left foot.

4. Cock your hands earlier on the backswing and take a normal swing down into the ball.

4. Ball in Divot or Bare Lie

1. Select a more-lofted club.

2. Position the ball slightly back in your stance with hands more forward than normal.

3. Swing down into the ball at a steeper-than-normal angle. Drive through the ball and follow through as much as possible.

4. From a completely bare lie, however, try to sweep the ball off the hard ground without taking a divot.

CHAPTER FIVE

Dialing in Your Short Game

Action without thought is a form of insanity; thought without action is a crime. —Albert Einstein

Golf is indeed a game of intellect. More than your physical prowess, it's the many minute-to-minute and day-to-day decisions you make both on and off the course that ultimately determine your destiny in this game. While the importance of on-course decisions is obvious to even the novice golfer, it is surprising how many golfers, some advanced, take a nonchalant, almost carefree approach to their golf training.

The biggest off-course decision you'll make relates to the frequency, methods, and the overall focus of your practice. This pith of this book is about helping you make the right decisions in each of these areas—in essence, "how to become a more intelligent golfer." Do so, and you'll stand out from the crowd and step up your game to the next level. Unfortunately, many golfers are handicapped by flawed decision making when it comes to practice. Some think practicing once a week is enough to improve, while others practice daily, but with antiquated or noneffective methods they're enamored of. Many golfers are guilty of training their strengths instead of their weaknesses—the classic example is the common mistake of overpracticing full-swing shots while largely ignoring the critical skills of the short game. If this sounds at all familiar, then it's vital that you apply the material in this chapter as a central part of your new—smarter—golf training program!

Putting for Dough

It's well known that putting practice is one of the fastest ways to lower your handicap. Despite this knowledge, few amateurs regularly train their putting in the same way they do their full-swing shots at the driving range. Make no mistake about it—there is no transfer of learning from full-swing shots to putting. Not three, five, or even ten hours per week spent at the range will have any impact on your putting game. The skills of swinging a club and putting are as different as kicking and passing a football. The only way to get good at both is through dedicated practice of both.

At the minimum, practice putting for thirty minutes, twice per week. This alone will lower your handicap if, like many golfers, you go from round to round without ever picking up your putter. As your skill increases, invest even more time, not less, on practicing your putting. Typically pros spend hours per week—sometimes per day—putting on the practice green with the intent of taking a stroke or two off their rounds in a tournament. While you probably don't have that kind of time to invest, you should strive for a 50 percent split of whatever practice time you have between your short game and full-swing shots.

The goal of putting practice is threefold: to develop feel for distance, to learn to read breaks, and to develop confidence. Since many amateurs neglect putting practice, they are essentially left to guess at the distance and break. Of course their confidence is, at best, modest, and their results are mediocre.

The *Golf Training* approach is to commit to regular practice knowing you'll learn to dial in even the most subtle breaks and develop a sixth sense for green speed. Clearly this will take time—you will encounter infinite combinations of speed and break on the links of the world. As described in chapter 2, however, the ability to approximate the correct solution to each unique putt can be acquired through the development of broad motor learning schemas. These schemas are road maps built into your nervous system through extensive practice over a wide range of conditions. Thus, lots of time spent on a single practice green limits learning. Upon acquiring beginner-level skill at putting, you need to expand your practice onto a wider variety of practice greens possessing different speeds and breaks. This highlights another good reason to travel to a different golf course every weekend— by starting and finishing each round with fifteen to thirty minutes of putting on the course's practice green, you'll code unique schemas into your skill map.

Putting Alignment and Setup

Golfers are as particular about their technique on the green as they are about their putters. Still, there are a few fundamentals to successful putting that you must abide by.

1. Read each putt as if it's for a tournament win. View the slope and break from off the green and then from behind the ball. Visualize the line or arc the ball needs to travel into the hole. Now trace that path from the cup back

to the ball and identify a start-to point over which you will roll the ball. The line from the ball to this start-to point defines the roll line along which you align your shoulders and square the putter face.

2. Your stance over the ball must be at a distance that places your eyes directly over the ball. Only this way can you accurately align the face of the putter perpendicular to the roll line. To check whether your eyes are indeed over the ball, take your putting stance, then have someone drop a spare ball from the bridge of your nose. The dropped ball should land on top of the ball you're putting.

Square the putter with the imaginary line extending from the ball to the start-to point, then align the feet, hips, and shoulders parallel to this line.

3. Your shoulders must be set parallel to the line on which you are starting the putt. Even a slight misalignment will result in a "push" or "pull" of the putt, and a long second putt.

4. You must relax through the shoulders, arms, and hands to heighten the sense of feel and control with the putter. Even the slightest tension can cause a not-so-slight miss.

5. The face of the putter must be square to the roll line along which the ball will start.

Personalizing Your Putting Technique

1. There are various grips used for putting, but the most common is the reverse overlapping grip, named for the overlapping of the left index finger over the right pinkie. The putting grip is one place it's all right to experiment and find what position feels best. For instance, many people extend their left index finger down the grip for added stability. No matter how you grip the putter, it is vital that your palms face each other and that the grip pressure remains light

and sensitive. Strive for a relaxed feeling all the way from your hands up through your forearms, upper arms, and shoulders.

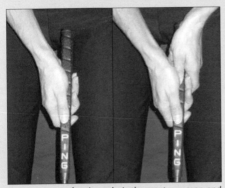

The **reverse overlapping grip** is the most common and intuitive putting grip.

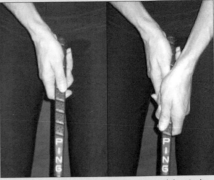

The **cross-handed grip** may feel less natural, but it does increase hand stability.

2. Foot stance should be parallel to the roll line or slightly open. Many people prefer a slightly open stance, which allows freer follow-through on longer putts. However, this can also throw your shoulder alignment off. If you start pulling putts, this could be your problem. Consequently, I encourage most beginners to square up both their feet and shoulders to the roll line.

Putting setup varies based on personal preference, but there are a few fundamentals such as *eyes over the ball* (left) and *hands set slightly ahead of the ball* (right) at address.

3. Spine angle and arm position vary widely among golfers, because they're largely determined by the length of the putter in use. The spine angle should be greater (more bend at the waist) than with the standard swing, and your arms should be at least slightly bent. Most important, find a position that encourages relaxation through your upper body while placing the putter head nicely behind the ball and your eyes over the ball.

4. Finally, there's your putter—the biggest personal touch you'll place on the putting game. Clearly, there is no best putter. It all comes down to what feels and looks comfortable. It might sound strange, but if you don't like the look of your putter you'll become tense and, of course, lack confidence. Feel is completely individual, so test out a wide variety of putters in the store and exchange a putter that doesn't groove after a few rounds. Conversely, when you find a putter that feels right, guard it with your life and don't mess with success.

The Putting Stroke

Quite simply, the arms move in a pendulum motion through the ball. The wrists remain fairly quiet and the lower body still throughout the putt. Make solid contact—the center of the clubface should impact the center of the ball with zero loft. Follow through a distance at least as far as your backswing. Finally, keep your head still throughout the putt. Many golfers mistakenly move their heads as they putt through the ball. I still hear my father telling me to "listen, don't look" for the ball to go into the hole. This practice might seem unnatural, but it's extremely effective.

The putting stroke is a pendulum swing with the hands, arms, and shoulders moving as a unit. Putting keys include quiet wrists, a still lower body and head, and a low, steady swing and slight acceleration through the ball.

The putting swing should be low to the ground and along the roll line. Use the same tempo for all putts regardless of length. Simply vary the size of the swing. As a rule for short putts, take the putter head back one inch for every foot of the putt (six inches back, for instance, for a six-foot putt). This prevents the common error of taking too big a swing on short putts and then decelerating at impact. In fact, the opposite is the ideal—a slight acceleration through the ball. Longer putts require more shoulder, which takes the putter inside on the backswing and follow-through. The putter face, however, must return to the square position at impact—this demands a stable, controlled stroke that you'll develop with regular practice. Use the drills on page 95 to foster good technique and the intuition needed for longer putts.

Cues for Putting

> Relax grip and feel the putter, eyes over ball, keep wrists and hands quiet, pendulum swing through ball, smooth and steady tempo, head still.

Pre-Putt Routine

In chapter 6 you will learn that preshot routines provide powerful anchors for peak performance. This applies big-time on the greens. Develop a ritual you go through before each putt and don't deviate. This lowers pressure, increases confidence, and maintains a rhythm you know works.

The following routine is a framework onto which to develop your personal ritual. Also, observe the preshot routines of pro golfers (this is one thing you can model from the pros). Even the most insignificant actions are actually part of the routine, such as the way Tiger cups the visor of his cap as he visualizes the putt. Experiment and discover what works best for you.

1. Begin your routine as you approach the green. View the overall slope of the green. Which way does it drain? Visualize successful 1- and 2-putts you've made on similar greens, or that same green if you've played it before.

2. Walk onto the green and view the putt from a few feet behind the ball. How do the small features of slope and break fit in with the overall slope you observed from off the green?

3. Visualize the line or arc the ball will travel into the cup. Now eye that line from the cup back to the ball and determine a start-to spot a few inches (short putts) to a few feet (long putts) ahead of the ball.

4. Set up near the ball and take a practice stroke or two. Intuit the degree of force your experience indicates you'll need for the putt.

5. Maintain steady breathing as you set up over the ball. Check the alignment of your shoulders to the roll line. Finally, double-check that the face of the putter is perpendicular to the roll line.

6. Again, visualize the line/arc the ball will travel to the cup and "see" the ball drop in. Refocus on the ball, relax, and take a confident stroke. Finally, to keep your head still on short putts, listen (don't look!) for the ball to fall into the cup.

Practicing Putting

Although the novice can learn the basics of setup and swing by putting on a carpeted floor, such blocked practice has little value for golfers with any experience. Effective practice must be variable in speed and break. The best indoor simulator is the Electronic Putting Challenge by GL Technology, which features seventy-two different breaks. Better yet, get outdoors and experience real conditions at a variety of practice greens and courses.

Beginners should focus on distance first and break second. Spend plenty of practice time around the hole performing the drills described below. The initial goal is to develop confidence on the green and a high rate of success from six feet and in. Over the course of a few weeks, expand your practice toward the edges of the green. Still, your focus should be on nailing correct distance over correct break. This approach and regular practice will make 3-putts a rarity on the course.

Five Key Drills to Improve Your Putting

1. Twelve-Foot Drill

This drill develops feel for the critical short- to medium-length putts you really need to hole. Place twelve balls in a straight line from the hole with each ball a foot apart. Therefore, the first ball is a foot from the hole and the twelfth ball is twelve feet from the hole. Sink the one-foot putt, then the two-foot putt, and so on. The goal is to get as many putts in the hole or within a one- to two-foot radius of the hole as you can. At first you may make only two or three of the putts. But repeat the drill a few times each session and you'll see rapid improvement as your feel for the distances increases. Keep a record of how well you do, and perform the drill during your next training session with the expectation of sinking at least one more putt.

2. The Cross Drill

This is classic variable practice that will surely have you reading break and distance better. Perform this drill in six stages with four balls or, ideally, with twenty-four balls preplaced in the proper position. Place the first four balls one foot from the hole at the clock positions of three, six, nine, and twelve o'clock. The next four balls are positioned one foot beyond the first set of balls. Do the same with a third, fourth, fifth, and sixth sets of balls. The complete setup is a cross extending about six feet out from the hole.

Begin by attempting the four one-foot putts. After making the putt from each of the four positions, move on to the two-foot putts. If you're using just four balls, retrieve the four balls from the cup and reposition them at the two-foot distance.

Upon sinking all four two-foot putts, continue on to the three-footers, four-footers, and so on. Take your time in visualizing and executing each putt—perform the same pre-putt routine before making the stroke. Not only does this drill develop your putting skills, but it also strengthens your focus and concentration skills. In time you'll gain a great sense of confidence all around the pin.

3. Long-Approach Drill

Golf is a game of near misses, and that's the strategy on long putts (greater than twenty feet). Although you will occasionally hole one from that distance, if you try too hard to make these long putts, it's common to overcompensate for the situation and leave yourself a long second putt. Thus, the best plan is to relax and simply try to putt the ball into the sure-thing range of three feet or less from the hole. Ideally, the putt will drop, but commonly you'll be left with an easy second putt in. As strange as it may seem, this strategy of "trying for a near miss" works best for most golfers.

This drill will acclimate you to this approach. Putt from a variety of locations around the practice green, mainly focusing on distances from twenty to forty feet. Pick a spot and hit as many balls as it takes to get one within a three-foot radius of the pin. Then move to another spot and, again, hit from there repeatedly until one stops within three feet of the hole. Initial use of this drill might require five or more putts from each spot to get the ball into the target zone. Over the course of a few weeks, however, your increased skill, confidence, and feel will have you putting into the target radius in one or two tries.

4. Eyes-Closed Drill

Just as the name says, you will practice making short putts (three feet and less) with your eyes closed. This simple drill works wonders for people with the bad habit of looking up too soon. Of course, looking up too soon creates undue movement in the upper body—often the reason people miss "give-me" putts.

Drop several balls at various spots within a three-foot radius of the hole. Perform your standard pre-putt routine, set up over the ball, then close your eyes before tapping the putt in. Don't open your eyes until you hear the ball drop in the hole (or until three seconds pass). Hit twenty such putts at the end of every putting session.

5. Putting Match

Here's a practice green game that is good fun and excellent training. Challenge a friend to a "round" of eighteen putts of varying distance and difficulty. Both of you hit one ball from the exact same spot, and the closest to the pin wins that hole. Flip a coin for who putts the first hole; after that, the loser of each hole putts first. Take turns picking the spot from which to putt—make the putts increasingly challenging in terms of both distance and break. Alternatively, you could play a round by yourself. Play eighteen different holes on the practice green, and play each through until the ball is drained. Write down the approximate starting distance (from the cup) for each hole and keep score as you go.

Chipping and Pitching to the Green

Chipping and pitching are the "up" skills of getting up and down. That is, a good chip or pitch shot up onto the green allows you the opportunity to sink a putt down the hole. The difference between these two fundamental shot types is the elevation and distance of the shot. Chip shots are low angle but with significant roll. A pitch shot flies the ball at a higher pitch (hence the name) and with backspin, the combined effect of which is little or no roll upon landing on the green.

As a rule your distance from the edge of the green and the pin placement determine whether you want to pitch or chip. You will want to pitch if it's more than about ten yards from the edge of the green or if the pin placement is near the front edge of the green. The chip shot is best from positions just off the green and when the pin placements allow enough room to run (roll) the ball toward the cup.

Chipping Basics

Of all the stroke-saving shots, the chip is arguably the easiest to learn because it's similar to the putting stroke. That's right, you're going to execute the same puttlike stroke for all chip shots, but vary the iron selected according to the length of the shot. A greater distance to the hole requires a less-lofted club—say, a 5-iron—which produces a lower, longer ball flight and more roll. A delicate ten-foot chip is stroked the same way, but with a pitching or sand wedge that will fly the ball just two or three feet followed by several feet of roll. This one-stroke style of chipping is more easily learned and maintained in the heat of play than the one-club method of chipping taught by some pros. The one-club method involves chipping with just one or two clubs, but with differing swing sizes depending on the length of the shot. I have worked with students who use both methods, and the one-stroke technique wins hands-down for ease of learning and reliability on the links.

As you might expect, the fundamentals of chipping are quite similar to those of putting. If you've worked through the putting drills from earlier in this chapter, you should have no problem hitting some clean chip shots during your first practice session.

Club Selection for Chipping

The three things to consider when determining which club to select for a chip shot are distance from the edge of the green, pin location, and the speed and slope of the green. Knowledge of these issues along with experience gained through dedicated chipping practices will develop a sixth sense at knowing just what needs to be done (and what club to select) in a given situation.

Earlier, I pointed out that the chip shot rules from most lies within ten yards of the green, while ball positions farther out usually require pitching. This is because only about a third of the distance a chip shot travels is in the air; the other two-thirds comes as roll on the green. Thus, chip shots from longer distances would require so much force and flight that the subsequent roll would send the ball off the back of the green. Even at distances less than ten yards, you may need to hit a short pitch if there's not enough space to roll it, as in a small green or front pin placement.

Mid- and back-green pin placements are ideal for chipping, because they provide plenty of room to roll the ball. Front pin placements can also be chipped to if you're only a few feet off the green. Again, consider the distance the ball must travel in the air to reach the green, and the fact that the ball will roll about double its flight distance.

Finally, you must factor in the slope and speed of the green. Novice golfers are always surprised to find how much difference in green speed there can be from one course to another. Just as in putting, chipping requires you to be a quick study at determining green speed and making the necessary adjustments. Obviously, the *one-third air flight, two-thirds roll* rule is an average. Uphill chips might result in half air flight and half roll, while downhill or fast greens could cause three or four times more roll than flight.

With all this in mind, select a sand wedge, pitching wedge, or 9-iron for the short chips and on fast greens. Medium-length chips with a total distance to the pin of ten to fifteen yards require an 8- or 7-iron. Finally, large or uphill greens with

Chip-and-Run to Back Pin Placement

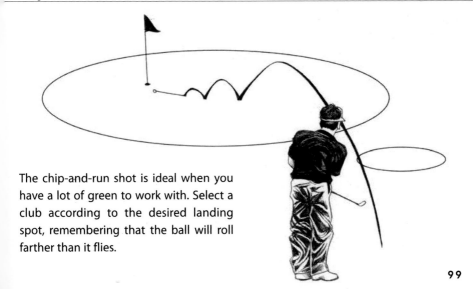

The chip-and-run shot is ideal when you have a lot of green to work with. Select a club according to the desired landing spot, remembering that the ball will roll farther than it flies.

99

Proper Chipping Technique

1. Visualize the shot you need to make based on your distance to the green, the pin placement, and the slope and break of the green. Identify the landing spot on the green from which the ball can roll to the pin. Aim at this spot.

2. Take a narrow stance with more weight on the left foot, and play the ball just in back of midstance. This will give you more of a descending blow, thus popping the ball up out of the longer grass.

3. Choke about halfway down on the grip for better feel and control. Some people like to use a putting grip for increased feel; you may want to experiment with this. Still, settle into one grip as soon as possible and stick with it.

4. Position your hands well forward of the ball to ensure proper loft of the clubface and solid contact.

5. Swing in "one piece"—that is, the hands, arms, and shoulder move back and through the ball with little wrist movement. Maintain more weight on the left foot with very little weight shift throughout the swing. Fewer moving parts mean a more consistent and reliable chipping stroke. Think *putt* as you execute the motion.

6. Keep your head down, and accelerate through the ball. Use a confident stroke as you would on a long putt.

far-back pin placements demand more force and, therefore, your 6- or 5-iron. Ultimately you'll need to log plenty of practice time to determine exactly how much distance you get out of chipping with each club.

Practicing Chipping

Although you could practice the chipping stroke in your backyard, you'll gain no knowledge of the results. A practice green is the ticket for effective chipping practice. Begin just off the fringe of the green and employ blocked practice to hit a series of short shots at a close pin placement. Here you'll be experimenting with your wedges and 9-iron to determine the distance you get from each. Your goal is to chip the ball to within two feet of the pin (I'm sure you'll hole a few in the process!) and to use the exact same stroke with every chip and with every club.

To expand your practice, move out from the green two yards at a time and hit to pin placements farther back on the green. Use your middle irons—you need both more flight (to the green) and more roll (on the green). Hit a few balls with the 8-, 7-, and 6-irons and note the average distance each club provides. Then pick a target and hit some shots with the goal of placing the ball within five feet of the pin. Change the club in your hands, not the swing, if you need more distance to reach the target. Certainly the longer chips are more difficult, requiring precise execution and feel. Use the less-lofted 6- and 5-irons, but maintain the same swing and resist the tendency to get "wristy" with the shot. Concentrate on keeping your hands ahead of the ball at impact, and think about moving the back of your left hand toward the target. This keeps the clubface delofted, producing the force (and distance) you need to make these long chips. Hit ten or twenty balls from this range, with the goal of getting to within five feet of the pin.

Cues for Chipping

Hands forward and firm, swing as in a long putt, low swing back and low swing through ball, pinch the ball, accelerate through impact.

Pitch and Lob Shots

Pitching skills must be on call for tight pin placements and at distances beyond twenty yards up around eighty yards, where your full-swing iron shots take over. These shots fly at a high trajectory and tend to stick on the green near where they hit. Tour pros hit these shots time and time again with remarkable accuracy, and it all looks so easy from the armchair. High-accuracy pitching is a skill that can be difficult to dial in. It'll likely take you a few seasons and hundreds of practice shots to dial in these skills and acquire the confidence and consistency you'll need on the course.

Pitching is fundamentally different from chipping. It's a two-lever system with more arm swing than chipping and more wrist cock. Also, you need to employ a little lower-body movement for added power and distance. What you end up with is basically a somewhat toned-down version of the full swing introduced in chapter 3.

Start out by training two different-sized partial swings for pitching. With respect to clock positions, work on a consistent five o'clock to seven o'clock swing (roughly thigh to thigh) and a larger, more wristy three o'clock to nine o'clock swing. In time you'll develop feel to execute in-between swings—say, four-to-eight o'clock—for any novel pitch you need to make on the course.

Five O'Clock to Seven O'Clock Pitching Swing

This shot is half chip and half pitch. The setup is much the same as for a chip—a narrow stance with more weight on the left foot, ball positioned center stance, and hands slightly forward of the ball—but the swing is a bit larger than in chipping and includes some hand cock and lower-body weight shift. Take the club back until your

Pitch to Tight Pin Placement

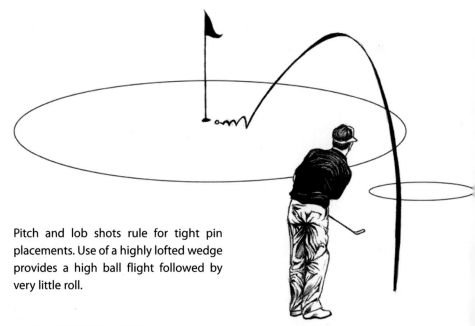

Pitch and lob shots rule for tight pin placements. Use of a highly lofted wedge provides a high ball flight followed by very little roll.

hands are near the five o'clock position, then accelerate through the ball and follow through to just beyond seven o'clock. Practice this shot with your pitching wedge and sand wedge, striving for a consistent swing that yields the same distance every time.

Three O'Clock to Nine O'Clock Pitching Swing

Longer pitches of forty to eighty yards demand a bigger swing with more torso turn and wrist cock. Assume a shoulder width stance, center the ball, and position your hands slightly ahead of the ball. Take a midsized swing with your hand fully cocking, your left thumb pointing toward the sky at the top of the backswing (hands at about the three o'clock position). Begin the downswing with a weight shift in the lower body, then uncoil and accelerate down through the ball. This swing should produce a divot and a follow-through to the nine o'clock position or beyond.

Practice these shots with the 9-iron, pitching wedge, and sand wedge. Concentrate on taking only the prescribed half swing—it's common to overswing and essentially take a full swing at the ball. Even worse, some people take too big a backswing (say, hands to eleven o'clock), then decelerate as they swing through the ball. A good follow-through is crucial to a successful shot, so it's better to swing through the whole way to a classic finish than pull up short.

Lob Shots

The lob is a soft, high-spin shot used to place the ball near a tight pin placement or to sit the ball on a fast green. These shots are hit with perfection by tour pros, but many amateurs struggle to hit consistent lobs. Some club manufacturers would like you to think that it's all in the club, but we know the truth—it's the archer, not the arrow! That said, you might want to experiment with one of these specialized wedges—though I believe you can also learn to hit effect lobs with your sand wedge. Here's how.

Address the ball with a slightly open stance, then open the clubface of your sand wedge by an equal amount. Position the ball forward in your stance, but shift your sternum over the ball by placing more weight on your left foot. This setup is similar to that used in bunker play, and you'll be taking the same steep swing down onto the ball. Vary the size of your swing and the degree to which you open the clubface to control the height and distance of your lob shots. Dedicate some quality practice time to hitting lobs and soon you'll be become confident in using them on the golf course.

Pitch and Lob Shots

Five O'Clock to Seven O'Clock Pitch: Set up using a narrow stance with more weight on your left foot. Position the ball center stance with your hands slightly ahead of the ball. Swing as in a long chip shot, but allow your hands to cock slightly and the lower-body weight to shift a bit through the swing. Accelerate through impact and follow through to beyond the seven o'clock position rather than pulling up short.

Three O'Clock to Nine O'Clock Pitch: Address the ball with a shoulder width stance, center or slightly back ball position, and your hands slightly ahead of the ball. Take what feels like a half swing, but allow your hands to fully cock. On the downswing, stay down on the ball by watching for the divot to appear from underneath the ball. Strive for a good, balanced follow-through.

Lob Shot: Address the ball with a slightly open stance, then open the clubface an equal amount to square the club to the target line. Position the ball forward in your stance, then shift your sternum over the ball by placing more weight on your left foot. On the backswing, allow the hands to cock more quickly, providing a steep-than-normal arc. Downswing along the body line, accelerate through the ball, and follow through high. Strive for the feeling that the club is sliding under the ball through impact.

Practicing Your Pitching

The strategy here is the same as in learning all the other golf skills. Practice the new skills early in the session while you're mentally and physically fresh; begin with blocked practice and progress to variable and random practice as you gain proficiency. The short game is all about feel, and it's not something you can rush. Take your training one success at a time.

Early sessions should focus on the easier-to-learn 9-iron and pitching wedge. Hit twenty or thirty balls with each from a perfect lie. As your five-to-seven-o'clock and three-to-nine-o'clock strokes solidify, introduce variable practice from more difficult lies as well as blocked practice with your sand wedge and lofted wedge. As a rule, though, save practice and play of these more difficult clubs for nearly perfect lies.

You can also train pitch shots in your backyard or at a park if the grass isn't too long. All you need is a bucket, a handful of balls, and your short irons. Place the bucket and step off a certain distance—say, twenty yards. Now practice precise five-to-seven-o'clock swings with each of the clubs and see which club provides the correct distance. Once identified, hit a series of blocked shots with that club, trying to get as many as possible in the bucket. You can also step off longer distances to practice, but be aware of innocent bystanders, buildings, and such.

Throughout all your practice, keep track of the distance that results from each swing and club. Otherwise, you might become an ace at pitching in practice but a failure on the course because you can't possibly manage your short game without an exact knowledge of your pitching distances.

Cues for Pitching

Relax arms and allow to dangle, soft hands, swing smoothly and modestly, stay down and watch for divot.

Getting Out of Bunkers

Sand shots are more intimidating than they are difficult. In fact, with the correct technique and some practice, you'll find getting out of a bunker to be one of the easiest golf skills to master. Unfortunately, the average golfer gets sweaty just thinking about a bunker shot! "Surely they are nicknamed *sand traps* for a reason?" Such fear of the sand leads to avoidance of bunker practice and, hence, unnecessary stress and multiple strokes when sand is encountered on the course. Sound familiar? If so, now is the time to end this overcharge in strokes by committing to regular sand-shot practice.

For the beginner, sand traps are a part of the game you can't avoid. You will either come to hate bunkers or learn to conquer them. Embrace the challenge, and commit to a minimum of at least one sand practice session per week. Do so, and soon you'll be hitting bunker shots like a pro. The formula to success is simple: Know the technique, practice it regularly, and play it with confidence.

Splashing Out of Greenside Bunkers

Greenside bunkers are the high-lipped, sandy encampments protecting the pin. Typically you'll need to hit very short shots, because the distance from the bunker to the pin is only a few yards up to, maybe, twenty yards in extreme cases. Also, the characteristically high lips require that you to get the ball up in the air faster to escape the trap. This combination of short shot and high flight should sound similar to the lob shot explained earlier. In fact, the swing is basically the same as with a lob shot; only the setup position and how you hit the ball change slightly.

On the latter subject, it is important to point out that you really don't hit the ball directly when executing a greenside bunker shot. The strategy is to hit a few inches behind the ball and blast it out atop a small cushion of sand. In most cases the specially designed sand wedge is the tool of choice. It has a wider sole (also called "bounce"), which weighs more and hangs down well below the leading edge of the

Open your stance and the clubface an equal amount so that the clubface has extra loft but remains square to the target line. Swing along your body line, however.

clubface. This feature allows the sand wedge to skid (or bounce) through a shallow layer of sand instead of digging in deep and getting stuck, as a normal club might. The extra weight at the sole also facilitates getting through the soft, loose sand in a smooth motion. Only if you come across a bunker with wet or hard-packed sand will you want to use a club with less bounce. In these situations, your pitching wedge would be the preferred club; the heavy sand itself will cause the club to skid under the ball while taking less sand.

It's important to note that most people struggle with sand shots not because they have the wrong club in their hands, but due to flawed setup and technique. Many amateurs attempt to use a standard on-the-grass setup and swing for sand shots, when in fact greenside bunker shots require a fundamentally different setup and swing.

Start by addressing the ball as usual, with your feet, body, and clubface square to the target line. Stand with the ball positioned forward in your stance and your club hovering three to four inches behind the ball. Now open the clubface so it aims about thirty degrees right of the target line and assume your normal grip on the club according to this skewed alignment. Correct this misalignment by opening your stance so your feet and body line point about thirty degrees left of the target. The clubface should now, again, be square to the target line, but with extra loft thanks

Greenside Bunker Setup and Swing

1. Address the ball as usual with your feet, body, and clubface square to the target line. Stand with the ball positioned inside the left foot (the ball should be forward in your stance) and the club hovering about three inches behind the ball. (Don't ground the club on the sand; this would cost you a penalty stroke during play.)

2. Open the clubface to aim about thirty degrees right of the target line, then take your normal grip. This delofts the club.

3. Now open your stance by moving your left foot (and the left side of your body) away from the target line so your body line points about thirty degrees left of the target. The clubface now should be square to the target line.

4. Check for hands positioned forward near the left thigh, and weight shifted slightly forward onto your left foot.

5. Relax throughout your body and, if you like, waggle your club a little. Maintain steady breathing; visualize the shot you want; be confident.

6. Focus on a spot in the sand about two or three inches behind the ball (farther back for shorter shorts). For initial practices, mark a spot in the sand behind the ball at which to look and swing.

7. Take a half to three-quarter pitchlike swing along your body line. The exact size and vigor of the swing is a "feel thing" you'll develop with practice. Initially it may help to think of swinging just hard enough to hit the sand the same distance you want the ball to fly in the air.

8. Follow through to roughly the nine o'clock position and finish with the back of your left hand facing the sky.

Cues for Greenside Bunkers

Relax, set hands forward, feel weight on left foot, focus on and swing at a spot behind the ball, splash through sand, follow through completely.

to the above procedure. Of course, you do not want to readjust your grip, but instead maintain the exact relationship between the open clubface and your body as created with this special bunker setup. Check to see if your hands are forward near the left thigh, and your weight slightly forward onto your left foot. Finally, relax throughout your body, and, if you like, waggle your club a little. Knowing that bunkers create tension, you must consciously counteract that tendency with steady breathing, a positive demeanor, quality visualization, and confident thoughts.

You are now ready for perfect extrication of your ball from the sand trap—first try! There are two vitally important things to bring about this reality. First, watch and swing at a spot two to three inches behind the ball; and second, swing the club along your body line, not along the target line. Granted, both of these things are easier said than done, since most other golf skills require you to look at the ball and swing toward the target. It is here where many people go wrong when hitting sand shots. They get the setup right, but the swing is wrong. Rest assured that with a little practice while you are mentally fresh, you will surely develop the concentration and skill to take a nearly perfect swing through the sand every time. It is just a matter of forming different swing habits for use in bunkers.

Finally, the size of the swing should be roughly three o'clock to nine o'clock, as performed in pitching. Take slightly less swing for close pin placements and fast greens and a bit more swing for shots that need to travel farther in the air. You can also regulate distance by taking more or less sand with your shot and by lofting or delofting your clubface. Most people quickly hone their bunker senses on these matters with a mere one hour per week playing in the sand.

Practicing Sand Shots

Practice sand shots for twenty to thirty minutes at a time. The common scenario of hitting just a handful of sand shots at the end of a practice session does nothing but ensure mediocrity in this aspect of the game. Hit a minimum of half a bucket of balls from a wide variety of lies. Begin by giving yourself perfect lies from the middle of the bunker. Hit from here until you feel your swing has grooved and your success rate and confidence are high. Then put your devious side to work, creating every kind of lie you could possibly imagine getting on the links. The common problem lies include down- and uphill, sidehill, plugged and "fried egg," and near-lip encounters. (The strategy for each is described on pages 112 and 113.) This type of practice can be great fun, and the payoff is monstrous confidence every time you encounter a bunker on the course. In time you'll agree: Sand shots are not really traps, but instead opportunities to accurately place your ball near the pin!

Hitting Out of Fairway Bunkers

Fairway bunkers are often just a minor inconvenience, frequently providing an easier shot than would the adjacent rough. The typical fairway bunker features a mainly flat surface and small lips. In such cases you would perform pretty much a normal swing with an iron or wood, just as you would on the fairway. The key here is making contact with the ball, not the sand, first. Since such a clean pickup off the sand is difficult, I advise selecting one club more (using a 5-iron, for instance, instead of a 6-iron) than you would normally use from that distance—if there's even a little sand between your clubface and the ball, it'll rob you of some yardage. Other than that, use a normal stance and alignment, swing smoothly through the ball (not into the sand behind it), and you'll find these shots relatively easy.

More difficult is a situation in which your ball lies near the lip of a fairway bunker. In this case you must forget about trying to make a shot to the green and instead focus on just getting the ball out of the bunker and into a good position on the fairway. To do this, simply treat the bunker shot as if you were in a greenside encounter. Use the precise greenside bunker technique described earlier.

Play fairway bunkers with a confident, decisive swing that picks the ball off the sand.

Techniques for Imperfect Bunker Lies

Unless otherwise noted, the basic setup, alignment, and swing are the same for these sand shots as detailed earlier. In most cases you only need to make a minor adjustment to accommodate the uneven lie. Consult the photos of uneven grass lies in chapter 4 (page 84) to see proper torso and shoulder position for first four lies described below.

1. Uphill Lie

Create a steady stance over the ball by swiveling your feet so they dig down a bit into the sand. This foundation supports a balanced, even swing. Now drop your right shoulder and tilt your body slightly to the right until your shoulder line parallels the slope of the sand. You will feel more weight on the right (downhill) foot—this is fine, but be sure your feet are dug in to help maintain your balance during the swing. Focus on a spot two to three inches behind the ball and swing with the slope (just as you would for an uphill grass lie), but along your body line.

2. Downhill Lie

Downhill slopes require a steep swing to get the ball up and out. Again, the method is about the same as with a downhill lie on the grass. Place the ball back in your stance, shift your weight more onto the left side (and keep it there), and shift your torso perpendicular to the slope. Swing with a strong, descending blow along your body line.

3. Sidehill Lies

Ball positions higher than your feet cause shots to fly slightly left of the target, and they can make you take more sand than you might like. To compensate, simply aim a little right of the target using the exact setup and swing for sand shots as described earlier. You'll want to shorten your club appropriately by choking down and/or standing up a little straighter than normal.

Ball positions lower than your feet require the opposite strategy. Aim a bit left of the target to compensate for the natural ball flight to the right. You'll also want to dig your feet into the sand and flex more at the knees and waist to prevent you from topping the ball. As always, focus and hit at a spot two to three inches behind the ball.

4. Plugged Lie and the "Fried Egg"

A plugged lie is when the ball has cored down into the sand, whereas a fried egg is when the ball is sitting down in a small crater but not buried. In both cases the ball is sitting below the surface plane of the sand, so the technique used is much different from other bunker shots. Begin by squaring your body and clubface to the target line—do not open your stance or the clubface as in the other bunker shots. The square clubface enables the leading edge of the clubhead to dig down under the ball, but at the same time it removes loft from the clubface and decreases the angle of ball flight. Therefore, it's vital that you take a fuller, more vigorous swing and strive to follow through toward the target. Do this, and you have a pretty good chance of extracting the ball from this difficult lie.

5. Bunker Lip Shots

If you are lucky, you will be faced with just a couple of near-lip lies each season. Such a lie can be very intimidating since there is little horizontal space to get the ball up and over the lip. Furthermore, the stance is as strange as they come in this game—typically you will need to have one foot on the grass and the other offset down in the sand. Here's how to get the ball up and out every time.

Take a square stance with your left foot up on the grass and your right in the bunker. Shift your weight forward onto the bent left leg as much as possible without feeling out of balance. Your right leg will be nearly straight and more lightly weighted. Square the clubface and position your hands well in front of the ball (the club-handle cap should be pointing toward the middle of your left thigh), but make sure the clubface remains square to the target line. The swing is all upper body, so keep your weight steady on the front leg. On the backswing, pick the club up toward the sky with less drag-back than usual. Swing *down* on the ball—not three inches behind, as in other bunker shots—and keep a firm left-hand grip so the club doesn't rotate in your hands during impact. Forget about trying to perform a normal follow-through; just stick the club into the sand behind the ball. End of swing. This action will pop the ball out at a steep angle and land it a few yards beyond the bunker. With practice, you will find that these shots are pretty easy.

Technique for Hitting Out of Fairway Bunkers

The following technique works for most fairway bunker shots with the typical low lip and flat lie. Encounters with steep lips or bad lies must be combated with the greenside bunker techniques described earlier.

1. Select a club one number lower (less lofted) than you would normally use from that distance.

2. Assume your standard address, except stand a slight bit taller or choke down a bit on the club. This helps prevent swinging into the sand before you get to the ball.

3. Focus on the ball and take what feels like a firm three-quarter swing. The goal is to make solid contact with the ball, not to kill it.

4. Follow through to a normal finish.

Cues for Fairway Bunkers

Relax as if it's a fairway shot, stand tall, swing like it's a fairway shot, focus on the ball not the sand, pick the ball off the sand, follow through naturally.

CHAPTER SIX

Winning the Head Games 6

Change your thoughts and you will change your world.
—Norman Vincent Peale

Your mind controls everything you do. Your mind *is* you! In sports, a properly programmed mind is tantamount to success; a poorly programmed one, to failure. Your mind is never neutral—it's either helping you or hurting you. Thus, it's paramount that you take control of your mind if you are ever to master this game.

Your mental skills are developed, maintained, and expanded in the same way you learn physical skills—through training and regular use. Such training, however, produces what appears to be less tangible results than, for example, skill training to hit lob shots. It is consequently overlooked, ignored, or even if practiced for a time, often quickly discarded as being less important than the obvious physical skills of golf.

Mental training requires discipline, which is why so few people do it. The goal is moment-to-moment awareness of the quality of your thinking: Is it helping or hurting you, is it goal-directed or fear-directed, is it compelling action or quelling action? Controlling your thoughts during practice sessions and every round of golf is not enough, because your focus before or between rounds or practice sessions can plant the seeds for success or failure. Consider Greg Norman's well-publicized collapse in the final round of the 1996 Masters. I believe he lost the tournament before stepping onto the first tee that Sunday due to poor-quality thinking in the hours leading up to the final round.

In this chapter I touch on nine elements of the head game. Although all are intertwined, I have broken them down into bite-sized pieces to be discussed in a logical progression. As you read, reflect on your own personal head games and consider what improvements can be made. Employ the tips found after each section to begin your journey toward the best golf of your life.

Motivation Multiplies Talent

Motivation is the foundation for all accomplishments. Natural talent, great genetics, and all the time and money in the world will get you nowhere without motivation. Many great human feats have been achieved by modestly talented, even disabled, people possessing heroic levels of motivation. Consider Oprah Winfrey running a full marathon or, on a deeper level, Ben Hogan coming back from a nearly fatal accident to win three majors in a season. Now, that's motivation!

It takes motivation to get out and practice after work or on days when the weather is less than ideal. It takes motivation to focus your practice on the weak areas you'd rather forget about instead of show to the world. It takes motivation to keep coming back to the game in the wake of a poor round. The fuel for this day-to-day and week-to-week motivation is your expectations, incentives, and goals.

First, it's important that you foster the expectation of success, whether you're at the practice range or on the golf course. At the range, expect that the practice session will increase your skill and elevate you toward your goals, no matter how good or bad it's going on any given day. On the links, expect to make a good shot every time; if you make a bad one, know that your chances of hitting a good shot on your next swing have just increased. No matter what the task at hand, there is a causal connection between believing in the best outcome and the likelihood that it will occur. This attitude stokes motivation and performance. Conversely, any thoughts that *Practice won't help* or *I'll never succeed* will lead to lower energy, lower motivation, and lackluster performance.

Incentives and goals also enhance motivation. Simple things such as a checklist of skills to practice, courses to play, a tournament you've entered, or a golf trip inked in on the calendar will maintain or elevate your motivation to practice. As the weak areas on your checklist improve, or as the tournament nears, your motivation will grow stronger still.

Finally, there's the power of visualization to motivate. Whether you're still learning the basic swing or practicing for a big tournament, visualization of the ideal outcome will power consistent actions throughout. Stephen R. Covey points out the importance of "beginning with the end in mind" in his book *The 7 Habits of Highly Effective People*. In this way, forming a vivid mental picture of the ideal outcome is a powerful technique for creating motivation and preprogramming success.

Training Tip

Cranking Up Your Confidence

As much as any other attribute, your level of confidence upon initiating a swing may predetermine your likelihood of producing the ideal outcome. As an example, consider your favorite hole on your home course—a hole you've played many times and admittedly have wired. As you prepare to play the hole, you probably feel no fear and possibly expect the results to be birdie or, at worst, par. You then proceed to play the hole in a relaxed, carefree, yet focused state and produce the results you expected. Such an experience depicts the dramatic effect confidence has on performance. But what exactly is confidence and how is it developed?

Confidence is positive energy, enthusiasm, and high expectancy of success. You play free, loose, fluid, and with good pace and rhythm—and even in the face of pressure, you remain mentally calm and focused. Such bulletproof confidence, however, does not just appear on the spot by thinking positive thoughts or hoping for the best. Confidence is developed beforehand via extensive preparation and experience. It is something for which you train.

As shown in the example above, nothing elicits confidence like having been there before. Accordingly, one of your training goals should be to mimic the atmospheres, situations, and terrains of the courses you play most often, or of the tournament course you will soon play. For instance, if you know you'll soon play a bunker-laden course, increase your practice of sand shots to fortify your confidence in this aspect of the game. Likewise, if uneven lies zap your confidence, go out of your way to play the most hilly course in your area several times. If playing under the pressure of competition is a problem, enter as many tournaments as you can for a full season. It will be money well spent, because the experience you gain in any of these situations accumulates and rewards you in the seasons to come.

You can also use your mind to bolster confidence in making a particular shot. Vividly visualize a similar past experience where you made a good shot. Reliving this past experience by actually *seeing* and *feeling* it again will transfer these resources for use in the present moment. This mental programming technique will increase your sense of certainty in the shot and crank up your confidence.

Training Tip

Confidence is essential to peak performance. Always acclimate yourself to the conditions, situation, and terrain you are most likely to come across in upcoming play. Mimic these conditions in practice, and if possible expose yourself to the exact conditions ahead of time in the form of a practice round or mock event. In both practicing and playing, maximize confidence by visualizing your proper execution in similar past situations, then visualize the ideal shot as it's about to happen—then let it happen!

Visualization—Preprogramming the Future

Name a great golfer of any generation—Byron Nelson, Ben Hogan, Jack Nicklaus, Nancy Lopez, Tiger Woods, Annika Sorenstam—and you are naming a master of visualization. While visualization is a fundamental skill used by top athletes the world over, it's also a powerful tool for beginner and intermediate athletes striving to learn new skills and enhance performance. For a golfer, honing your visualization skills is just as important as refining your swing skills. Better play requires both.

Recognize that visualization goes beyond the simple task of reviewing the hole and sighting the shot. As used by all peak performers, visualization is vivid, extremely detailed, mental moviemaking that preprograms future reality in the brain. This form of mental training helps improve mind–body integration and enhances your feel and execution. Your mental movies are, in fact, blueprints for action, so be sure they are positive and accurate. Surely, some bad performances have been preprogrammed through unclear or negative mental imagery.

Use visualization before every shot or putt, and in every practice session or round you play. Not only will this improve the overall quality of your practice, but it will make you a Zen master of visualization in the heat of competition. Take your time and make your mental movies complete with sound, color, and kinesthetic feel. Start by examining the details of the lie and alignment, then make and view your movie of the desired shot. Take one practice swing and feel the shot, then step up to the ball and let it happen. Clearly, visualization should be incorporated as part of your preshot routine (to be discussed later in this chapter).

Another use of visualization is in preparation of playing an unfamiliar course. If available, buy the course's yardage book and mentally play through it, hole by hole. In the case of tournament play, schedule a practice round or at least do a quick walk-through of the course. View the fairway, hazards, and greens from several angles to gain as much information about the layout and dynamics of the course as you can. If possible, take notes along the way, and load up on as much input as you can squeeze out of local players—does a certain hole play "long," or is there a specific hazard that's troubling for players of your ability? The world's best golfers are masters at seeing a course just once or twice and then quickly creating a detailed movie of playing a successful round. This mental movie, played repeatedly, helps program their future reality.

A final use of visualization in sports is mental "practice" of skills on rest days or while laid up due to injury. Even though your body is at rest, you can exercise your brain's motor (skill) programs by visualizing their execution as you would see and feel it in action. Studies have shown that this helps maintain sports skills even during lengthy layoffs. You can employ this rest-day mental training while away on business trips, during times of illness or injury, or during a long, cold northern winter. This practice is certainly more beneficial than doing nothing at all.

Tips to Supercharge Your Visualization and Performance

Visualization helps preprogram future realities, so use it in all aspects of your life—at home, at work, and in any activity at which you desire excellence. Here are six tips to make your visualization most effective:

1. Practice visualization with all your senses and create images in explicit detail. The more vivid the images, the more powerful the effect visualization will have on your performance.

2. Gather information with a walk-through or practice round, or by studying a yardage book or the course overview on the scorecard. If possible, talk to locals who can give firsthand knowledge of how the course plays.

Putting demands sharp visualization skills. Get down low and *see* the line.

3. Use visualization before every shot, whether at practice or play. Mental and physical practice combined produces better results than physical practice alone.

4. Create and store positive images for recall in countering negative pictures, thoughts, or feelings that might crop up as you play.

5. Create mental movies of yourself dealing with various situations or problems that might arise on the course.

6. Work every day to supplant negative and self-defeating images (in any activity) with positive and constructive counterparts.

Anchoring Performances with Rituals and Routines

Pre-round rituals and preshot routines are powerful anchors for consistent performance. Whether it's an exact sequence of activities and a "to-bed" time for the day before a tournament or a mental checklist of preshot actions and thoughts, consistent rituals yield highly consistent results.

Develop rituals for the days and hours leading up to the start of a round based on past experiences. What did you do and think in the minutes leading up to some of your particularly brilliant rounds? What did you do the day before that helped maximize your energy and mental state? Awareness of all the little things is key, including meals, warm-up routine, whom you did or didn't talk to, how and when you prepared your equipment, and even what music you listened to. The more detailed and lengthy the rituals, the greater the effect.

Novice golfers with little playing experience don't need to start from scratch. Employ the preparations and adopt the attitude you possessed before some of your better practice sessions. Also, talk to some more experienced golfers to find out what rituals have worked for them. Ultimately, you need to log some rounds of golf and experiment with your preparatory routine. Through acute awareness you'll eventually notice some causal connections between your pre-round rituals and the outcome on the course. In the seasons to come, you'll refine your rituals as your game itself is refined.

Rituals are especially useful as time markers leading up to the start of a tournament. The ritual may begin days before the event and count down to the minutes before the tee-off, as you perform your warm-up, stretching, visualization, and preparatory self-talk. Stepping up to the first tee, your focus will be laserlike and your confidence high knowing that your tried-and-true rituals have placed you in the ideal performance state of past successes.

Preshot routines are similarly effective at producing the physical and mental environment needed for peak performance, and they are ubiquitous among elite athletes. Whether it's Serena Williams preparing to serve or Barry Bonds stepping up to the plate, every serve or swing is preceded by an identical preparatory routine. Every tiny detail is programmed into a mental checklist, including posture, breathing, visualization, and final thoughts. For these athletes, habitual rituals help produce the consistently positive results that have made them world famous.

In chapter 3 I provided you with an outline for an effective preshot routine. Of course you'll want to personalize the sequence, and shorten it over time to just a few key steps. Similarly, you want a unique routine for use before every putt, as discussed in chapter 5. Make the routines exact and use them every time you address the ball, whether at the range, on the practice green, or on the course. Infrequent use of rituals and routines essentially short-circuits the anchor and diminishes its efficacy in later use. If you are too tired or rushed to use your rituals and routines, then call it a day rather than mess with success.

Training Tip

Consistent rituals and routines give birth to consistent performances. Establish a detailed pre-round ritual, including all activities from preparing your equipment and body for play to preparing your mind and strategy for the course. When the ritual becomes tried and true, stick to it! Preshot routines should be highly refined for use in the moments leading up to each shot. Include everything from sighting the shot, to taking your practice swing and setup, to your visualization and final swing thought.

Fear: The Enemy Within

Fear kills performance. Period. In golf, the common killers are fear of failure and fear of embarrassment—and, at the elite level, fear of success. There are also subconscious, preprogrammed fears that are the root of many of the dumb things that seem to "just happen." Have you ever missed a gimme putt or botched an approach shot from your best distance? It may be that such mistakes are the result of unchallenged inner fears, since lack of ability can be ruled out.

Deal with your fears head-on beginning today. Start by writing down recurrent fears that clearly hurt your performance. If you can't think of any on the spot, go play a round and pay special attention to every pre-swing thought and between-shot concern. As the fears reveal themselves, use logic, reason, and statistics to specifically counter each. For instance, as you set up to make an over-water shot, quell fears of hitting into the water with the knowledge that you have plenty of club to clear the hazard if it's a good shot, and that a good shot is most probable. Or if a 3-putt on the last hole has raised fears as you step up to putt out the next, consider that in light of your average of 1.8 putts per hole (or whatever), the odds of either a 2- or 1-putt are now stacked in your favor.

Dealing with fear is an ongoing process, because our fears are ever-changing. Upon completing a poor round of golf, always analyze what went wrong and try to identify what fear(s) may have contributed to your difficulties. To help you with this analysis, here's a primer on two of the most common fears in this sport: fear of failure and fear of embarrassment.

Fear of Failure

This deep-seated fear is instilled during childhood, when family and teachers tend to classify all our actions as either good or bad, success or failure. As kids we've all been in situations where the fear of failure was so gripping that we became immobilized and time seemed to stop. Fortunately, adults generally don't react quite that intensely, though it is still common for us to imagine all the bad things that could possibly go wrong. Once triggered, these negative thoughts can snowball and, more often than not, become self-fulfilling prophecies.

In golf, fear of failure causes you to hold back. Your attack on a course becomes less aggressive than required, your swing weakens and tempo changes, you find yourself second-guessing a shot or club selection as you stand over the ball, and your breathing becomes shallow and muscles tighten. You may even fall prey to paralysis by analysis, freezing over the ball or even whiffing.

Eliminate fear of failure in one of two ways. First, focus on what is probable instead of what is possible. Sure, it's human nature to always consider the worst-case scenario, but it almost never happens. Counter these thoughts by considering what is probable and realistic based on past experiences. The second method to nix this fear is to focus all your attention on the process of playing the game and forget about the possible outcomes. Concentrate on the things immediate to your performance, like making a perfect setup and releasing tension. Visualize crisp, colorful images of the shot you want to make, and then let it happen that way.

Supplant fearful thoughts of the hazard with confident, process-oriented thinking.

Remember, in sports there are no failures, only results. If you slice a drive or miss a putt, it is the result of poor concentration, poor mechanics, or a poor read, not because you are a worthless individual. The results might not be ideal, but they do contain hints for improvement. It is through your failures that you grow as a golfer and a person. This is one of the classic ways in which golf imitates life!

Fear of Embarrassment

Fear of embarrassment or being dissed by other golfers is insidious. Nip it in the bud today; otherwise you will forever be controlled by others. This fear also guarantees that you'll never be able to fully enjoy this sport and most certainly won't reach your potential. The first step is to leave your ego at home and walk onto the practice range or course determined to play *your* game. What others might think or say cannot enter your mind, or your performance will be compromised.

Realize that occasional bad-performance days are inevitable. Instead of trying to avoid them, simply accept that they happen, analyze why they happened, then bury them. With this attitude, you will be free to try chancy shots, go for the pin, or pull out the driver and risk an occasional mistake. In the long run you'll become a better, more confident golfer, and more often look like a hero than a zero. Likewise, don't let fear of looking like a wimp keep you from hitting, say, a 5-wood off the tee or laying up on the second shot of a par-4 if this is the best play for you. It should always come down to playing your game, not someone else's.

When contemplating a potentially embarrassing situation, remember that your friends know how good a golfer you are, and they won't think any worse of you because of a poor shot, round, or tournament. Any strangers who might be critical of your play simply don't matter and aren't worth a millisecond of your precious time. Work on improving your self-confidence and don't let the criticisms of others invade your thoughts. A common characteristic of peak performers in all walks of life is that of being habitual doers who can tune out the critics. Turn the "critic receiver" off—play your game and live your life.

Training Tip

Write down your golf course fears, then challenge them head-on. Confidence and reason are the antidotes to most of these fears. Focus on what is probable and not on the less likely worst-case scenario. When faced with a hazard, acknowledge that the course designer placed it there to create fear, then laugh at it and use your experience and skill to navigate successfully by it. To possess the fear is to fall into the designer's trap—figuratively and literally.

Turning Down the Pressure

Pressure is not inherently good or bad. It's your ability to control and react to pressure that determines its value. You've probably experienced high-pressure situations where nervousness, anxiety, tightness, and lack of focus prevailed, ultimately dooming your performance. Times like these make you yearn for no-pressure situations—surely that would be the ideal. Right?

Well, actually not. Some degree of pressure is good, and many pros like to feel the butterflies born out of pressure going into a round. Moderate pressure fosters an energy level and degree of focus that is quite productive for many performers. Remember the pressure of cramming the days and nights before a major exam or important sales pitch? Moderate pressure acts as a bit of a stick and when combined with a tasty carrot (the goal), the results can be stellar. The key is learning to use this "good" pressure, and eliminate externally generated "bad" pressure.

The control knob to pressure is completely in your hands. Realize that while you will never have control over all elements of a situation, you do have control over your reactions to them. Psychologists explain that no one makes you feel pressure, fear, anger, or frustration but you. Either you allow yourself to feel that way, or you empower someone else to make you feel that way. Acknowledge that you are at the helm of your emotions. Work for constant awareness of how you feel and why. Only then can you make the necessary changes that will give birth to optimal performances.

Let's consider a few ways to optimize pressure in stressful on-the-course situations. The goal is to maintain positive pressures that originate from within, while eliminating negative pressures that are typically external.

Positive pressure evolves from effective preparations leading up to the round or event and knowledge that the goal (to win, to shoot in the 80s, to break 100, or what have you) is attainable if you play your best. For instance, a good week at the range, a great practice round or warm-up, proper rest, and a good support team will leave you anticipating a solid, successful performance. You'll be focused and optimistic, and ready to get on the course and play your best. Such positive pressure is the antithesis of the anxiety and bad attitude that can result from poor preparations, a rushed warm-up, too little sleep, and hanging out with negative people.

Training Tip

Moderate pressure, not no pressure, produces peak performance. Strive for acute awareness of what you are thinking and how it's affecting the pressure you are feeling. Use visualization and relaxation as an antidote to bad pressure you're feeling, but accept and embrace good pressure as an ally to performing your best. (Use the Relaxation Sequence on page 128.)

Controlling Focus

Most people think about focus as a narrowing of concentration. In fact, the act of focusing can be either a laserlike concentration of mental energy on a single object (such as the ball) or a broad-beam scan of the fairway and hazards ahead. Like using a camera with a zoom lens, however, you must deliberately zoom in and out, composing your field of view in the most productive way. The key word here is *deliberate,* since mental focus is an act. Too many golfers lack the ability to focus their attention deliberately and consistently. Some aim at a general area instead of a

Relaxation Sequence

Perform the following procedure at least once a day, ideally in a quiet, dimly lit room. Allow fifteen minutes at first, but with practice you'll be able to reach a state of complete relaxation in less than five minutes. This sequence requires you to tense, then relax various muscles in your body. Note the difference in feeling in a tense versus a completely relaxed muscle. The goal is to develop awareness of different levels of muscular tension as well as the ability to release high levels of it.

Proceed through the sequence in this exact order, flexing only the muscle(s) specified in each step (a valuable skill you will master quickly). Perform the sequence lying or sitting in a comfortable position. Spend about one minute on each step.

1. With your eyes closed, take five deep belly breaths. Inhale slowly over five seconds, then exhale to a silent ten count.

2. Tense the muscles in your lower legs (one leg at a time) for five seconds. Let go of the contraction and feel the tension release. Focus on total relaxation of the muscles; feel them become light and airy.

3. Now do the same sequence with the muscles of the upper leg. Tense only those muscles and hold for five seconds. Relax and feel the tension drain away. Remain focused on the relaxed feeling of the muscles. Do not let your thoughts stray. After a minute move on to the next body part.

4. The arms are next, starting below the elbow. Make a tight fist for five seconds, then release. Allow your fingers and hands to fall completely relaxed.

5. Now tense the muscles of the upper arm, one at a time. Try to tense/relax the biceps and triceps separately. Spend at least one minute on this step.

6. Next, tense the muscles of the torso for five seconds, then relax. As you get better, try to tense the chest, shoulder, back, and abdominal muscles separately.

7. Finish by tensing the muscles of the face and neck. Then relax them completely, focusing on the complete feeling of relaxation that develops.

8. Concentrate on relaxing all the muscles in your body. Mentally scan from head to toe for any muscles that might still contain tension. Maintain this state of total relaxation for at least three minutes.

9. Open your eyes, stretch and feel refreshed, or begin visualization training. If you're tired, take a nap.

specific target, while others stare out-of-focus at a fuzzy space around the ball instead of the ball itself. Let's sort things out.

The most difficult part of focus is learning to zoom in and out quickly from a pinpoint focus to a more wide-angle perspective and then back. The wide-angle mode is used when viewing the fairway or green area ahead in developing a strategy. You then need to zoom in on the exact target to which you want to hit the ball. Now you zoom back out, viewing the line of flight you'd like the ball to travel to the target area. Finally, you zoom in on the ball, and then take your swing. Throughout this process you need to ward off outside distractions that threaten to grab and divert your focus. This is the biggest problem for many golfers, because their focus is easily diverted by what people around them are doing, background noises, or even their own thoughts of the eventual shot outcome. Therefore, part of effective focus is the ability to redirect your attention onto the task at hand, while letting go of everything else.

Like your other golf skills, focus is best trained at the driving range and practice green. After a warm-up period, hit a series of shots to several different driving-range targets with a variety of clubs. Practice focus as discussed above: first a wide-angle view of the (imaginary) fairway ahead, next a tight zoom-in on the specific target, then a wider view of the desired path to the target, and finally a pinpoint focus on the ball. Repeat this process with every shot, and place as little focus as possible on your swing mechanics and your surroundings. Be the ball!

This exercise is indeed difficult. Your thoughts undoubtedly will wander to what other golfers around you are doing, and your focus may turn to critical self-analysis after a poor shot. When this occurs, simply redirect your focus back to this training exercise and continue on. A key part of this drill is the sharpening of your awareness of when focus is lost, and developing the ability to return it to the desired task.

The same drill should be used on the practice green. With a wide-angle focus, view the green's topography to diagnose major features that will produce break. Next, focus on the pin and scan back toward the ball, noting more subtle irregularities and identifying a spot toward which you want to start the ball. Finally, you zoom in on the ball and putt.

Practice this focus exercise every visit to the range for a month. As your mental endurance increases, you'll be able to increase the length of time you can maintain the focus. Eventually, effective focus will become part of your routine and almost completely second nature.

Training Tip

Focus enhances the mind's connection to the process of getting the ball to the target and, thus, the odds that it will. Commit a few weeks to actively training focus as you practice. After approximately ten focus training sessions, the focusing process will become nearly automatic. Keep training it until it becomes an inseparable part of your preshot routine.

Maintaining Control and Poise

Emotional control in sports, also called poise, is fundamental to optimal performance. Dealing with pressure before a round (as discussed earlier) is a good start, but controlling emotion as you play is just as important and often much more difficult. Ultimately, you must be able to rein in your emotions and react constructively to any errors or misfortunes that occur along the way. Otherwise you'll forever be stuck playing far below your true potential.

It's natural for nervous energy and emotions to rise as you play golf, a sport with so much break time between plays. Believe me, it happens to the very best. It's how you deal with it and how often you regulate your arousal that determine whether it will negatively impact your performance.

The key to maintaining control is a one- to two-minute mental break from the game after each shot. Spend these breaks thinking and talking about anything but the game at hand. Pick light subjects such as sports, movies, or whatever puts you in a good mood. This loose, happy break time helps zero out your emotions and tensions before you begin to work on the next shot.

In highly tense situations where a break isn't possible, employ the ANSWER Sequence to aid in gathering yourself for the upcoming shot. This sequence is a simple, effective means of maintaining complete control of your mind and body in the midst of high-drama play. It involves a deliberate directing of your thoughts inward (and away from play for a moment) to check and adjust your breathing and level of muscular tensions and to counter any self-defeating thoughts. Scan your body for any undesirable changes—say, rapid breathing, overgripping of the club, or tightening of the muscles—that have taken place since the last break or centering. Make immediate corrections before the problem snowballs and destroys your optimal mental and physical state for performance. Golfers who succumb in these situations are obvious—they become spastic, spew curses, and throw clubs.

The ANSWER Sequence

This six-step procedure will initially take a few minutes to perform. With practice, however, you'll be able to go through the sequence in about ten seconds—perfect for use before high-pressure golf shots or any other time you want to control tension.

Step 1. Awareness of rising tension, anxiety, or negative thoughts.

Acute awareness of unfavorable mental and physical changes is fundamental to optimal sports performance. It takes a conscious effort to turn your thoughts away from the outer world and toward your inner world. Peak performers habitually make these tension checks every few minutes. Make this your goal.

Step 2. Normalize breathing.

Golf is not an aerobic activity. Your breathing should be as relaxed as it would be when walking around your home. Unfortunately, many golfers hold their breath during setup for a swing, then breathe heavily afterward to catch their breath. This process creates tension and will sabotage performance. Your goal is smooth, even, normal breathing.

Step 3. Scan for specific areas of muscular tension.

Scan all your muscles in a quick sweep to locate pockets of tightness. Commonly tight areas for golfers are the forearms (do you overgrip your club?), shoulders, upper and lower back, upper legs, and calves. The best way to relax a specific muscle is to consciously contract it for about two seconds, then relax it and concentrate on the feeling of the tension draining from that muscle (visualize air escaping from a balloon).

Step 4. Wave of relaxation.

Upon completing the tension check above, take a single deep breath and feel a wave of relaxation wash from your head to your toes.

Step 5. Erase thoughts of past events (or the future) and focus on the present.

This step involves freeing your mind from the ball-and-chain of being outside the moment. There is no benefit to pondering the last putt that lipped out or the last hole on which you double-bogeyed. Let go of the past shots just as you let go of each passing breath. Refocus on the present, visualize the ideal shot, and believe in it.

Step 6. Reset your posture and flash a smile.

It is amazing how much positive energy you can generate simply by resetting your posture and smiling. This final step will leave you in an ideal performance state for setting up to make your next great shot. Trust your skills and let it happen.

Practice ANSWER at home, work, the range, or anytime you need to rein in your emotions and lower tension. As with any skill, you need to practice regularly to become proficient in its use. Soon you'll be able to reset your emotions in just a few seconds, regardless of the on-course or off-course situation.

Training Tip

Controlling emotions as you play is tantamount to controlling your perform-ance outcome. Take the game one shot at a time, and always indulge in a one- or two-minute mental break between shots. In the most high-tension situations, perform the ANSWER Sequence to reset your emotions and renew your optimal performance state for next crucial shot.

Self-Talk Yourself to Success

Much of this chapter has been about increasing awareness of mind and body. Neither can be ignored; they are inseparable and intimately affect each other. A simple example of this is that birdie-putt jitters can make you anxious, just as anxiety can give the jitters. To combat this inside-out or outside-in self-destruction, you've been presented with several effective tools such as the ANSWER Sequence, visualization, preshot rituals, and focus training. Lastly, I will cover a powerful self-management tool called *self-talk*. Whether you are aware of it or not, self-talk is something you undoubtedly already engage in. The goal, however, is *conscious* use of self-talk, and it's paramount to maximizing performance.

We think in pictures and words. The pictures we see and the words we say are the seeds of reality. Earlier I discussed the importance of making mental movies via visualization. This last section is about tuning in to the constant chatter of words in your head and how you can use it to affect reality as well. This is your self-talk.

Become a personal spin doctor by using your self-talk to best manage setbacks and challenges.

Self-talk can affect sports success as much as any other part of your life. As an example, let's consider two golfers of equal skill but vastly different self-talk. Before attempting the same difficult tee shot on a long par-3, they each think:

Golfer A	Golfer B
The pin placement is awful.	*The pin placement looks challenging.*
I hope I don't slice.	*Odds are I hit a good shot.*
The bunkers in front of the green look wicked.	*I have plenty of club to hit the green.*
The crosswind makes this shot even harder.	*The breeze feels good. I'll adjust my aim.*
Many people are watching me.	*Focus on the process, not the outcome.*

Which golfer do you think will perform better? Golfer A is indulging himself in negative, worrisome self-talk that plants the seeds for poor performance. Meanwhile, golfer B is using self-talk to affirm her preparedness and to spin the upside to the weather and her shot-making statistics. Your goal is to emulate the positive approach of golfer B and ward off the negative psyche of golfer A. Let's look at both.

Negative self-talk is insidious because you may have been engaging in it for so long that you're unaware of it or even think it's normal. Thus, becoming aware of all your self-talk at home, school, work, and while playing golf is the first step. Next, you must supplant the negative talk with optimistic talk and positive spin. Be aware, however, that drowning yourself in false positives holds no value. For instance, if you can't hit your driver at the range, it is farcical to tell yourself you can do it on the course.

Effective self-talk is affirmation of your preparedness and positive attributes, not hopes or wishes of what you want to happen. Like golfer B, your self-talk should relate to positives in the reality of the given situation. Confirm why you should do well.

Many top athletes actively use self-talk as they perform to enhance focus, remind themselves of fundamental skills, and counter false negative thoughts. All your swing thoughts and cue words are indeed self-talk. But what are you saying to yourself in addition to your typical swing thoughts? Tune in and take note, because many golfers' pre-swing thoughts contain self-defeating messages. Also, keep your self-talk going after each shot in the form of affirmations. Again, they have to be valid thoughts to be effective; there's no upside to telling yourself a shot into the trees was a "great shot." Instead, use self-talk to get back into a controlled, confident state with statements like *I've been here before and survived* or *I can punch it low through the trees and still save par.* Of course, the worst thing you can do (and it's quite common) is beat yourself up with negative self-talk. That won't change the shot—nor will it help you play any better from there onward.

Like your muscles, your mental state is constantly in flux—either you're building it up or tearing it down. Always base your self-talk on what you have, not on what you don't have, and keep it focused on the present not the past. The long-term aggregate influence of changing your self-talk will be a seismic shift in the quality of your golf and your life!

Training Tip

Positive self-talk enhances your overall mental state and odds of success. Use self-talk to counter negative thoughts, cue swing skills, and reinforce your positive qualities. Engage in positive self-talk throughout the day and in all aspects of your life—you *cannot* just turn it on when you hit the links. Strive to become a personal spin doctor by using self-talk to deal with whatever challenge you face. The words and pictures you dwell on set the stage for your future realities.

Mental Wings Strategies for Uncommon Success

To conclude this chapter, I'm happy to provide a primer on my husband's Mental Wings™ program for uncommon success. These Mental Wings strategies can be used to enhance your performance in any activity or aspect of your life, and applied to golf they are some of the most powerful stroke-shaving techniques presented in this book. Following are five Mental Wings strategies you can begin using to today. To learn more about the complete Mental Wings program, visit *www.MentalWings.com*.

Strategy 1: Separate your self-image from your performance.

If you are reading this book, then golf surely plays a major role in your life. Unfortunately, when your self-image is tied too strongly or singly to this role, it translates to an overwhelming need to perform perfectly every time in order to prove your worth in that role and, thus, as a person. The subsequent pressure can become stifling; it may be the single greatest cause of frustration in this sport (or in any endeavor).

Human beings perform best in a process-oriented, not outcome-oriented, frame of mind. Detaching your self-image from your golf performance allows you to enjoy

The biggest secret to better golf is to separate your self-image from your performance and to love the game unconditionally.

the process of golfing regardless of the outcome. More important, it liberates you to try new shots or attack a course because you'll be able to deal with a poor shot, should it happen. In this way, self-image detachment will reduce pressure and anxiety—and paradoxically, you'll golf better by not needing to!

Strategy 2: Surround yourself with positive people.

There is an aura of influence that surrounds each of us, and its effects are based on our personality and attitude toward life and its events. Your thoughts and actions will affect the thoughts and actions of those around you, and vice versa.

As I see it, there are three options—either golf alone, golf with upbeat and positive people, or golf with cynical and negative people. Why would you ever want to go golfing with the complainers out there? Their negative aura will negatively impact your quality of play and enjoyment, whether you recognize it or not. Vow to either golf only with positive individuals or by yourself—both approaches can be hugely rewarding.

Strategy 3: Get into the peak performance zone.

"The zone" is an internal state where everything comes together for the perfect shot or personal-best round, and it all seems to happen almost effortlessly and automatically. The trick is being able to create this state on demand and often in stressful situations, such as at a competition or when playing a course for the first time. The best way to do this is by using one or more of your senses to reenact the feelings of a brilliant performance or event from your past (this doesn't necessarily have to be a golfing event). Have you ever experienced the relaxed pleasure that washes over your mind and body when you hear an old song or smell something familiar that instantly connects you to a great event in your past? That's what you're after.

If you've been golfing many years, then you surely have some "perfect" past days you can use as anchors for your peak performance state. If not, think back and identify some other event where you felt like you were in complete control and that anything was possible. Create about a sixty-second mental movie of this past event using all your senses. Make the pictures crisp and bright, and let the feeling and state of that event take over your body. Some people find that listening to a particular song through headphones is a powerful anchor for locking in the peak performance state. Be creative and experiment in developing you own preperformance rituals that can transport you into the zone.

Strategy 4: Leverage a "mental scrapbook" of past successes to persist through adversity.

This fourth strategy is extremely powerful, and it's fundamental to achieving high levels of success in any field. Create a mental scrapbook of past successes that you can review on demand to fortify your confidence and persevere in the face of apparent failure. Relive in your mind's eye the process of some of your greatest accomplishments, both golfing and nongolfing. Make these mental movies vivid and get inside them as if they were happening again at the present moment. *Feel* the exhilaration and joy of the accomplishment, then take that emotion and apply it to the difficult situation with which you are presently faced. Forge ahead wearing the "mental armor" of your past successes and a whole new level of performance will begin to be revealed.

Strategy 5: Be happy regardless of situations and outcomes.

A superior trait of all real winners is resilience to bad results and/or criticism and unwavering belief that success will come with time, effort, and patience. Attitude is the wild card in the golf performance equation that can often compensate for what you are lacking in skill or experience. I can't overstate the importance of always having fun. We all take to golfing because we love the outdoor experience and the feeling of hitting the ball, yet in time far too many golfers become tense and miserable if they aren't hitting it perfectly every time.

The biggest secret to better golf is to love golf unconditionally. Vow that any day out golfing is a great day regardless of the results, and you will usually get the results you desire.

CHAPTER SEVEN

Fitness Training and Performance Nutrition

7

We first make our habits, then our habits make us.
—John Dryden

It is hard to image the words *strength training, performance nutrition,* and *aerobic training* ever being uttered in the context of a conversation regarding ways to improve golf performance. After all, golf requires mastery of complex motor skills and the mental domain, not brute physical strength. Just think about golf's greatest players over the years—their physiques hardly compare to those of other sports icons such as Michael Jordan, Barry Bonds, or Lance Armstrong. But times are changing, as are the players of this great game.

Picture Tiger Woods's physique, then observe his play. Having done this, many amateurs and pros have run—not walked—to the gym to start fitness training! It's no secret that fitness workouts have long been a part of Tiger's golf training program; in fact, many of the tour's rising stars have made a habit of keeping in shape. As for the tour veterans, they are either shaping up or shipping out.

The benefits of getting in shape for golf include decreased risk of injury, increased endurance, more carry distance, and a greater sense of confidence. But as in training your technical skills, there is a right way and a wrong way to go about training your golf muscles. The use of strength training programs designed for other sports will be ineffective and could produce negative results for golfers. Your fitness training game plan must be both sport-specific and properly tailored to your level of performance on the course. Coming right up, I'll show you the way to get started—but please consult a physician first if you have any doubts about your ability to participate safely in an exercise program.

Improved dietary surveillance is the other half of shaping up for golf. Besides supplying the building blocks for your muscles, a proper diet provides the right fuel and nutrients to keep your mind and body performing efficiently throughout a long round of play. Nobody would consider choking a high-performance German car with low-end fuel, yet many golfers pump junk food into their bodies and then wonder why they choke on the last few holes on the course. Some foods exhibit subtle druglike effects that can decrease mental and physical performance, whereas other foods can help maintain concentration and steady energy. I will present this information in a simple, easy-to-use way by utilizing a food-energy index that distinguishes high-performance foods from performance-killing foods. But first, let's take a look at fitness training for better golf.

Fitness Training for Golf

There are two types of fitness training programs: general and sport-specific. The goal of general training is all-around conditioning of the neuromuscular and cardiovascular systems, whereas sport-specific training focuses directly on strengthening the muscles and motions of the golf swing. Sport-specific training is the winning ticket for already in-shape and mid- to low-handicap players, while out-of-shape or novice golfers will benefit more from general fitness conditioning.

Before I cast off into a primer on general training, I want to stress that no amount of fitness training will bring about improvements on the course anywhere comparable to the benefits accrued from regular practice at a driving range or putting green. Make no mistake about it, the fitness training described in this chapter is a supplement to, not a replacement for, your outdoor golf skills practice.

General Conditioning

To determine your need for general conditioning, review your score in the physical fitness portion of the chapter 1's Self-Assessment Test. Out of the possible 30 points, a score of 20 or less signals your need of some fitness training. You can confirm this result by answering the additional five questions below. A yes answer to any question indicates that such training is appropriate.

1. Do you experience lower-back or elbow pain during periods of regular practice or play?

2. Are your practice sessions or play on the course (especially the back nine) affected by increasing physical fatigue?

3. Are you overweight for your body size? Use the "pinch-an-inch" test (actually a good measure). If you can pinch more than an inch-thick fold anywhere around your midsection, then you're overweight.

4. Does tightness in your shoulders, torso, lower back, or legs preclude you from executing a full and proper swing?

5. Are you noticeably fatigued the day after a long practice session or round?

The three prongs to the general conditioning program are stretching to improve flexibility, aerobic training to reduce body fat and improve cardiovascular endurance, and weight lifting to strengthen the major muscle groups. A basic workout covering all three aspects can be performed in less than sixty minutes at a local health club. Always execute the workout in the order described above: stretching, aerobics, strength training.

Stretching

The following eleven stretches serve as an excellent warm-up for the rest of your workout. Preworkout stretching improves the quality of your training, lowers perceived exertion, and may reduce the risk of injury during the workout. When performed daily, these stretches also will increase your flexibility, making for an easier-feeling swing and greater range of motion. More important, a limber body carries less tension—something from which every golfer can benefit. But to reap these benefits you must commit to a minimum of ten minutes of stretching every day, whether it's a golf day, fitness training day, or rest day.

Hold each stretch for between ten and twenty seconds and slowly exhale as you gradually increase the pressure of the stretch. Then relax, take a breath, and repeat. Never bounce your stretches; such ballistic stretching only makes a muscle tighter and risks injury. You can, however, safely double the length and volume of your rest-day stretching by doing up to four sets of each stretch and by holding them for up to thirty seconds. Stretch both sides of your body equally.

Eleven Tension-Relieving and Muscle Warming Stretches

1. Knee to Chest (lower back & hips)

This stretch feels good because it loosens the often tense muscles of the lower back. Lie flat on the floor and pull one knee toward your chest while keeping the other leg straight. As a variation you can pull your knee across your body toward the opposite shoulder to also stretch the outside of the hip.

2. Spinal Twist (lower back & hips)

Sit with one leg flat on the floor and the other bent and crossed over the flat leg. Place the elbow opposite the bent leg on the outside of the bent leg. Turn gently at the hips as if to look over your shoulder—but don't force this stretch beyond the point of mild tension. Hold for ten to twenty seconds and repeat.

3. Sit and Reach (back of legs)

Sit erect on the floor with your legs straight out in front of you. Cross one leg over the other, placing the foot of the bent leg on the outside of the straight knee. Now lean forward and reach for the toes of your straight leg. You can aid the stretch by wrapping your arms around the bent leg and pulling your chest and stomach toward the thigh of the bent leg.

4. Seal Stretch (abdominals)

Perform this stretch carefully, particularly if you have lower-back problems. Lie stomach-down on the floor with your hands palms-down on the floor in front of your face. Now press your upper torso up away from the floor until you feel light stretching of your abdominal muscles—at the same time contract your buttocks to limit stress on the lower back. Hold the stretch for ten to twenty second.

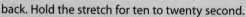
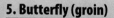

5. Butterfly (groin)

Sit on the floor erect and place the soles of your feet together a comfortable distance from your crotch. Grab hold of the laces side of your shoes and rest your elbows on your leg just above the knees. Maintaining a straight back, lean forward

and apply light pressure on your legs with your elbows.

6. Finger Walk (upper arms, shoulders, and back)

Sit on the floor with your legs bent about halfway and feet flat on the floor. Position your hands directly behind the hips with arms straight, palms flat, and fingers pointing back. Slowly walk your fingers backward from your hips until you feel tension in your chest, shoulders, and biceps.

7. Leg Curl (upper legs, shins, and hips)

Stand with one hand on a wall (or holding on to a solid object) for support. With the free hand, reach behind your back and grab your foot as you curl it up toward your buttocks. Hold firmly on to the toe of the shoe and gently pull upward to increase the tension of the stretch.

8. Side Lean (upper arms, upper back, and abdominals)

Standing with arms overhead and bent at the elbows, grab one elbow and pull it behind your head until you feel a stretch in the triceps and shoulder. Now slowly lean sideways in the direction of the stretch to extend that stretched feeling down your side toward the hips.

9. Arm Pull Across Chest (shoulders and upper back)

Pull your elbows across your chest, each toward the opposite shoulder. While still pulling, slowly move your elbow up and down to work the complete stretch.

10. Overhead Reach (forearms, upper arms, and shoulders)

Stand erect with your arms crossed above your head and palms facing each other. Push your hands slowly upward and back to increase the tension of the stretch from the hands to shoulders.

11. Wrist Curl (forearms and wrists)

Stand with your hands extended straight out to the front and palms facing each other. Bend one wrist inward and with the other hand gradually increase the wrist flex until you feel the stretching from the back of your wrist up to the outside of your elbow.

Aerobic Training

The compelling reasons for aerobic exercise are to lose weight and strengthen your cardiovascular (CV) system. Body fat above the normal range of 10 to 18 percent has multiple downsides, including undue stress on the bones, joints, muscles, connective tissues, and heart. Additional downsides for the golfer are reduced range of motion, compromised technique, and premature fatigue. A poor CV system results in rapid fatigue and diminished play during the course of a normal round of golf. Worse yet, it increases the chance your life will come to a premature end.

Now let's view the flip side, since positives are often more motivating than negatives. If you want to swing better, play with vim and vigor throughout those long four- to five-hour rounds, score lower, and increase your life span, get started with some aerobic training today. (You also will want to examine your diet for changes that can be made—see the "Diet and Performance Nutrition" section later in this chapter.)

General Strength Training

An excellent general strength training workout can be performed at any reasonably outfitted health club or spa. If you already belong to such a club, you're in luck; if not, join one near your home or place of work. It doesn't have to be the best or biggest—ease of access is key. (Odds are you'll rarely make the trek if you can't get there in less than fifteen minutes.) All the facility really needs is a circuit of Nautilus, Cybex, or similar machines and a couple of the aerobics options named on page 145. Fancy computerized machines are not necessary, nor are traditional free weights.

Aerobic Training for Better Health and Performance

The goal is to perform fifteen to thirty minutes of an aerobic exercise that elevates your heart rate to between 65 and 85 percent of maximum. Estimate your maximum heart rate by taking 220 minus your age. For example, a thirty-five-year-old has a maximum heart rate of 185 beats per minute, and 65 to 85 percent of this maximum rate gives an optimal aerobic training zone of 120 to 157 beats per minute.

You get maximum benefit from your aerobic exercise by maintaining a heart rate within this zone for the full duration of exercise. No matter the method, increase the intensity or speed of training if your heart rate is below this zone. Conversely, you should slow down when your heart rate exceeds the high end of the training zone. The easiest way to monitor your heart rate is to take a fifteen-second heartbeat count from your wrist and multiply by four. Do this every three to five minutes during your aerobic exercise.

Regular aerobic training will improve your stamina on the links, as long as your chosen training activity is rigorous enough to make you breathe heavy and break a sweat.

The best exercises for aerobic training are brisk walking, stationary biking, stair climbing, rowing machine, swimming laps, Rollerblading, and running. Exercises that involve many different muscle groups (such as rowing, swimming, and power walking) are much harder than those in which you are just moving your legs (like a stationary bike). Begin with the easier exercises, then graduate to more intense activities as your conditioning improves. I personally favor fast walking or running in the great outdoors. If your lower back and knees are healthy, buy a good pair of running shoes and hit the roads or trails. Otherwise, choose one of the low-impact exercises mentioned above. Finally, avoid the gimmicky "sliders" and "gliders" advertised on TV. As a rule, no-sweat workouts (an oxymoron) provide little effect other than to lighten your wallet.

The purpose for this strength training is not to build big muscles or lift heavy weights. The goal is to tone all the major muscle groups, giving you a more sound foundation from which to execute the golf swing while reducing your chance of a sports-related injury. Furthermore, toned-up muscles burn more calories around the clock as well as yielding an overall sense of well-being and confidence. You can gain all these upsides from a modest time investment of about twenty-five minutes, three days per week. Warm up for your strength training exercises with ten to fifteen minutes of stretching and twenty minutes of aerobics. All totaled, you are looking at a one-hour workout that will enhance your health, golf performance, and longevity!

Initial workouts will require a little experimentation to determine the appropriate training weight for each strength training exercise. The ideal weight will allow you to perform ten to fifteen repetitions before reaching muscular failure. Perform the repetitions in a controlled and slow manner, with each up-and-down movement taking about two seconds—count "one one-thousand, two one-thousand"—to complete.

Upon finding the correct exercise weight on each machine, stick with it until your newfound strength enables you to crank out more than fifteen reps. Then simply increase the weight by five to ten pounds for the next workout. Keep a written record of your weights and reps so you can track your improvements. Seeing the gains in black and white helps stoke the fires for future workouts. Finally, if you have selected enough weight to produce failure in the suggested range of reps, you

Strength Training Exercises to Enhance General Fitness

Listed below are twelve basic strength exercises you'll want to perform. Enlist an instructor or personal trainer if you are unsure about the lifting machines or proper technique needed for each exercise.

Bench press   Leg press
Shoulder press   Leg extension
Lat pull-down   Leg curl
Upright rows   Rotary torso
Triceps pushdowns   Back extension
Reverse wrist curls   Abdominal crunches

do not need to perform a second set. Only highly trained individuals need the extra stimulation of a second set to bring about the desired training effect.

Sport-Specific Training

While general strength training is essentially a traditional health club workout, sport-specific training targets the muscles and motions specific to golf. This very focused type of training is not appropriate for out-of-shape or novice golfers—these individuals should spend all their supplemental training time on aerobic conditioning, stretching, and general strength training. For the more experienced golfer, however, such sport-specific training is one of the keys to attaining the next level of performance.

An exercise is sport-specific (actually, golf-specific) only if it trains a muscle as it is used in the golf swing or if the exercise motion mimics part or all of the swing. Consequently, such exercises can directly increase your clubhead speed and distance, while general exercises will not. Still, I recommend you perform a full general workout after finishing up with the golf-specific exercises below.

I'll describe two types of golf-specific exercises: swing-weight club exercises and free-weight exercises. Your skill level and the facilities available determine which method is for you.

Swing Training Exercises

Swing-weight training involves performing the swing drills described in chapter 3 (see pages 56–59) with a half-pound weight added to the end of a club. As you swing the club, this added resistance builds golf-specific strength and clubhead speed. It's the same training principle that baseball players utilize when adding weight to their bats during warm-up swings.

Swing-weight exercises provide the most specific muscular training for golfers, since they stress the swing muscles as they are used when hitting a ball. The limiting factor, however, is that you can add only a small amount of weight to your club (any more than half a pound is not advised), thus limiting your potential to build strength. What's more, such weighted-swing exercises can compromise or even worsen a not-so-well-grooved swing. Consequently, the novice or struggling golfer should perform these drills without adding weight to the club.

Perform these swing training exercises during the winter off season or year-round to strengthen your swing and add distance to your game. For in-season practice, carry a half-pound swing weight in your golf bag so you can do five to ten minutes of swing-weight exercises as part of your range practice. I suggest saving swing-weight exercises for an end-of-practice coup de grâce, although you could perform a few repetitions as part of your warm-up (just don't overdo it). Please note that if you are ever short on practice time, it would be best to skip the swing-weight exercises completely rather than reduce the length of actual golf skills practice.

Off-season (winter) swing-weight training requires a room with a ceiling high enough to perform an uninhibited swing. The typical house ceiling isn't high enough. Your health club or a local gymnasium is the best bet, because these facilities almost always have ten-foot or higher ceilings. Otherwise, locate a golf store with a simulator or swing area in which you can buy thirty-minute increments of practice time.

Golf-Specific Free-Weight Training

Golf-specific free-weight exercises are the gold standard for serious strengthening of the "golf muscles." These exercises will not affect your swing mechanics, but the progressive nature of this training will produce noticeable strength gains that translate to the swing.

For right-handed golfers, these exercises focus on the left side of your body (of

Swing-Weight Training Exercises

These five swing-weight exercises can be performed with or without a swing weight. Initially, it's best to learn each exercise using one of your woods and no weight. Add a half-pound swing weight as the movement grooves and as you begin to feel comfortable in the execution of each exercise. Consult pages 56–59 in chapter 3 for photos and descriptions of each exercise. Perform one or two sets of each swing exercise, up to three days per week.

Preset Turning Drill

Feet-Together Drill

One-and-a-Half-Arm Drill

Post-Impact Extension Drill

Weight-Shift Swing Drill

course, left-handers train the right side). For muscle balance, however, perform these exercises on both sides of your body, with the exception of the dumbbell swing and left-arm cable pull. Always err on the side of using too little weight, since you are more likely to cheat on the exercise motion and use poor technique if the weight is too heavy.

Due to the fatiguing nature of these exercises, limit yourself to one maintenance workout per week during the season. Train for gains during the off season with a three-days-per-week schedule of golf-specific weight training. Always begin with a warm-up that comprises stretching and some aerobics. Ideally, you will perform the complete suite of stretching exercises along with fifteen to thirty minutes of aerobic training before beginning your free-weight exercises. Feel free to take a five-minute rest before moving onto the golf-specific free-weight exercises. Save any general weight training exercises—squats, bench presses, and the like—for the end of your workout.

Finally, if at all possible, continue to swing a club at least once per week during this off-season strength training program. Motor learning studies have shown it is useful to combine some skill training with such strength training, especially for less skilled athletes. Even just thirty minutes per week of indoor swinging will help maintain or even improve muscle memory during the off season.

Golf-Specific Free-Weight Exercises

1. Reverse Wrist Curl

This forearm-strengthening exercise should be performed year-round, because it's highly effective for preventing an injury called lateral epicondylitis, better known as golfer's elbow. Use a five- or ten-pound dumbbell and position your forearm horizontally (either on a bench or with the opposite hand supporting it) with the palm facing down. Begin with the wrist in the neutral (straight) position,  and curl the weight upward as far as possible. Lower to the neutral position (not below) and repeat. Perform two sets of about twenty-five reps with each hand.

2. Triceps Kickbacks

It's fundamental that the left arm leads the force-producing downswing, and this exercise helps strengthen the muscles of the upper arm. With a wide, balanced stance, bend over and rest your right arm on your right knee. Using a moderately heavy dumbbell in your left hand (held close to your chest, with arm bent), press it back beyond your hip until your arm is straight. Do two sets of ten to fifteen reps with both

arms. Begin with a five- to ten-pound dumbbell and increase weight as needed.

3. Bent-Over Lateral Dumbbell Raise

These dumbbell raises strengthen shoulder and upper-back muscles specific to golf. Use a wide and slightly staggered stance, bend at the waist, and place your right hand on your right knee. Holding a dumbbell in your left hand, raise the weight up to your side until it's parallel to the floor; hold it there for three seconds. Lower the weight slowly and repeat this motion for ten to fifteen reps. The weight should be heavy enough to make the last few reps difficult without compromising form (keep your arm straight). Do one to two sets on both sides.

4. Abdominal Crunches

This, too, is a must-do exercise for all golfers. Strong abdominals provide better support for the lower back as well as helping transfer lower-body energy to your upper body and, ultimately, the club. Lie flat on the floor and elevate your knees either by placing your lower legs on the seat of a chair or by holding your bent legs off the floor with your knees positioned over your hips. Cross your hands over your upper chest so that your elbows point toward the knees. Now raise your shoulders and

upper back off the floor just far enough to touch your elbows to your thighs. Alternatively, position your hands lightly behind your head but do not interlace your fingers or pull on your neck or head. Do two to four sets of as many reps as possible (until failure).

5. Dumbbell Swing

This exercise strengthens all the muscles used in a golf swing, from your forearms to your shoulders, back, and legs. Assume a normal golf stance with a light dumbbell in  your left hand. Perform a normal swing in every way—but much slower—keeping your head down through the impact zone. Then follow through completely. Do two sets of ten to fifteen repetitions. Begin with a three- or five-pound dumbbell, and take it easy.

6. Left-Arm Cable Pull

This exercise strengthens many of the muscles that uncoil to power the downswing. Take a normal golf stance in the middle of a cable cross-through machine (standard at most health clubs). Grab the top right handle with your left hand—your shoulders should be turned as if you were in the midst of a backswing. Pull down and through as similarly to a normal swing as possible. Slowly lower the weight back to the  start position and repeat ten to fifteen times. Use a very light weight for this exercise. Begin with ten pounds, then progress on to fifteen and twenty pounds over the course of several months.

Diet and Performance Nutrition for Better Golf

Proper nutrition plays a peripheral, yet influential role in performance, whether you're a beginner or scratch golfer, in shape or out of shape. Certainly even the soundest diet in the world won't take strokes off your game if you're not practicing; however, if you are doing everything else correctly, improved nutrition will give you an extra edge. Not surprisingly, many professional athletes, including some tour pros, regularly consult with nutritionists. The most common subjects of interest are how to modify diet to lower body fat; how to maintain consistent energy levels during a long, stressful competition; and what to eat and drink (and what to avoid) to maximize mental performance. I'll conclude this chapter with a primer on each of these important topics.

Lowering Body Fat

You could open a library if you owned all the books written on this topic. Ironically, weight loss is not that complex a subject; I'll cover the fundamentals here in just a few pages. Let's get started with two ironclad absolutes regarding weight loss.

Absolute 1: To lose weight, your daily calorie intake must be less than your total calorie expenditure for the twenty-four-hour period. Regardless of where the calories come from (fat, carbohydrate, protein, or alcohol), your daily net must be negative.

Absolute 2: "Diets" don't work. Whether you stay on them for a week, month, or year, you will gain all the weight back when you go off the diet. This is exactly what happens to 90 percent of people who try to lose weight. The 10 percent who lose weight and keep it off aren't "on a diet"; instead they have made fundamental changes in the way they eat that are *permanent*.

To begin, you need to change your nutritional paradigm. The Four Food Group nutritional model, taught in school for most of the twentieth century, is antiquated. The new, sounder model is a Nutritional Pyramid that places more emphasis on fruits, vegetables, pasta, and whole grains. These carbohydrate-type foods form the foundation of the pyramid, as they should your diet. Meanwhile, the smaller upper levels of the pyramid represent the animal and dairy products, oils, and sweets that must be deemphasized if you're going to lose weight.

Nutritional Pyramid: A Guide to Daily Food Choices

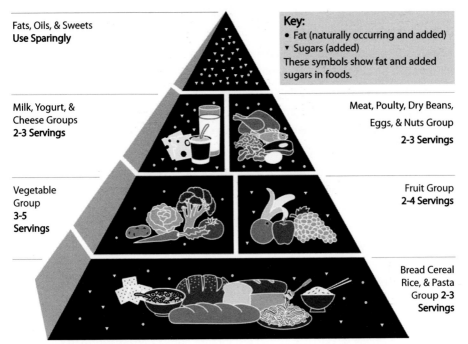

Fats, Oils, & Sweets
Use Sparingly

Key:
• Fat (naturally occurring and added)
▼ Sugars (added)
These symbols show fat and added sugars in foods.

Milk, Yogurt, &
Cheese Groups
2-3 Servings

Meat, Poulty, Dry Beans,
Eggs, & Nuts Group
2-3 Servings

Vegetable
Group
**3-5
Servings**

Fruit Group
2-4 Servings

Bread Cereal
Rice, & Pasta
Group **2-3
Servings**

Source: U.S. Department of Agricultural/U.S. Department of Health and Human Resources

Calculating Calories

Let's start with the fact that a gram of fat contains nine calories of energy, while a gram of protein and a gram of carbohydrate contain just four calories each. It's easy to see that reducing the amount of fatty foods in your diet will lower your calorie intake more than twice as much as cutting back the same amount on carbohydrates or protein. Thus, the simplest step toward dropping some unwanted pounds is to swear off high-fat foods. When you do eat dairy and animal products, select the low-fat versions. For instance, drink skim milk and eat grilled chicken or extra-lean cuts of steak instead of the typical whole milk, fried chicken, burgers, and pan-style pizza.

Overall, total calories consumed for the day when separated according to the three macronutrients should be about 60 percent calories from carbohydrates, 20 percent from protein, and 20 percent or less from fat. Unfortunately, the fast foods and highly processed foods so popular today nearly reverse these numbers, thus inverting the Nutritional Pyramid. For example, a McDonald's meal of a Big Mac

Ten Strategies for Weight Loss and More Healthful Nutrition

Following is a table of ten highly effective strategies for making permanent dietary changes to optimize your body composition and improve your overall health.

1. Always eat breakfast. You will perform better throughout the day, increase your metabolism, and avoid extreme hunger and resultant overeating.

2. Consume a modest dinner, and don't eat any food within three hours of bedtime. Consider the feeling of slight hunger before turning in for the night as a sign you are on target, not a signal that you need a snack.

3. Favor water or diet sodas over sugar-filled, nondiet beverages. Limit alcohol consumption to just a couple of drinks, once or twice per week. Alcohol contains nine empty calories per gram.

4. Read food labels. Avoid both high-fat and high-sugar foods. Select foods that fit the 60/20/20 carbohydrate/protein/fat profile. (See "Calculating Calories.") Eliminate from your diet all foods containing hydrogenated oils—found in almost all highly processed foods or products packaged for long shelf life. These trans fats, as they are called, are performance killers and may be cancer causing.

5. Reduce intake of added fats. Butter, salad dressings, oils, sauces, gravies, and such can contain up to ten grams of fat (ninety calories) per tablespoon. Select low-fat versions whenever possible and, at restaurants, order salad dressing and sauces on the side (so you can regulate the damage).

6. Eat more fish and poultry, and less red meat. Ask for your chicken and fish to be grilled or baked, but never fried. Select water-packed tuna and use "lite" mayo in the preparation. For red meats, select the leanest cuts and trim off the fatty pieces.

7. Eat only low-fat dairy products. Despite what you may have heard, skim milk is healthy as long as you are not lactose intolerant. Drink up to four glasses per day of this low-fat, high-protein "super food." Nonfat yogurt is also excellent.

8. Order only veggie or plain pizzas—meat toppings or extra cheese are nutritional disasters—and limit yourself to eating just two or three slices. Order thin crust (not pan-fried or Sicilian) and ask the pizza chef to go light on the cheese. Do all this, and pizza is not the bad food that some people claim.

9. Favor carbohydrates with a Glycemic Index of less than 70. (For more about the Glycemic Index, see page 156.) You can't go wrong by selecting whole-grain breads and lots of fresh fruits and vegetables. Eat up!

10. Save calorie-dense pleasure foods as infrequent rewards for an especially good workout or round of golf. At restaurants, consume only a salad with low-fat dressing for dinner if you plan to treat yourself with a decadent dessert. Cakes, ice cream, most croissants, and muffins contain large amounts of fat and sugar—a single serving can contain nearly a meal's worth of calories.

Determining Caloric Needs, Ideal Calorie Profile, & Weight-Loss Prescription

1. Your caloric needs are a function of your metabolic rate, body weight, and the amount and intensity of exercise you perform. Estimate your daily caloric requirement as follows:

    a. • If you have a slow metabolism, multiply your body weight by twelve. This is your daily "maintenance" caloric need.
        • If you have a midrange metabolism, multiply your body weight by fifteen.
        • If you have a high metabolism, then multiply your body weight by eighteen.
    b. Add 150 calories for each hour of low-intensity exercise you perform. Therefore, walking a four-hour round of golf burns about six hundred extra calories for the day. Of course, using a cart lowers this number markedly. High-intensity exercise can burn five hundred calories or more per hour. Therefore, thirty minutes on a stair climber or stationary bike burns about 250 calories more than the base amount calculated above.

    As an example, a 170-pound person with a midrange metabolism who walks a four-hour round would burn roughly: (170 x 15) + 600 = 3,150 calories on that day.

2. Determine your calories consumed for the day by tracking the number of grams of the three macronutrients contained in each food. Doing this for a full week every few months is a great way to maintain awareness of the foods you are eating and the macronutrient profile of your total diet.

    Suppose the same 170-pound golfer eats the following of each macronutrient:

    • 450 grams of carbohydrates at 4 calories per gram = 1,800 calories
    • 100 grams of protein at 4 calories per gram = 400 calories
    • 55 grams of fat at nine calories per gram = 495 calories

    The calorie total for the day is 2,695, with a macronutrient profile of 67 percent carbohydrate, 15 percent protein, and 18 percent of total calories from fat. This ratio is quite good since it's not far from the ideal 60/20/20 ratio described earlier.

Weight Loss Tip

As we all know (and as the above example shows), losing weight is a slow, difficult process. Doing it right requires a good offense (exercise to burn calories) and a good defense (controlling food intake and avoiding calorie-dense fatty foods), as well as persistence and vigilance. The best road to weight loss is to achieve a high frequency of near-five-hundred-calorie-deficit days. Larger daily deficits will leave you weak, excessively hungry, and more likely to break your diet with a binge.

Glycemic Index of Common Foods

High (>70)		Medium (50–70)		Low (<50)	
Bagel	72	Banana	~55	Bulgur	48
Carrots	71	Bran muffin	60	Spaghetti	41
Corn chips	73	Oatmeal	61	Whole wheat	37
Cornflakes	77	Raisins	64	All-Bran	42
Doughnuts	76	Rice	56	Orange	43
Honey	73	Sweet potato	54	Pear	36
Jelly beans	80	Wheat crackers	67	Apple	38
Potatoes	83	Cookies	~60	Peas	48
Rice (instant)	90	Sucrose	65	Baked beans	48
Rice cakes	82	Soft drink	68	Lentils	29
Rice Krispies	82	Orange juice	57	Milk (skim)	32
Grape-Nut Flakes	80	Granola bars	61	Fructose	23
Cracker (soda/water)	~76	Macaroni	64	Grapefruit	23
Glucose	100	Shredded wheat	58	Yogurt (w/ fruit)	~30
Gatorade	78	Ice cream	~60	Peanuts	14
Clif Bar	~70	Powerbar	~65	Balance Bar	~30

or nine-piece Chicken McNuggets and french fries breaks down to roughly 35/15/50 for carbohydrate, protein, and fat, respectively. Methods for approximating your personal caloric requirements and for calculating your ideal macronutrient breakdown are detailed in the box on page 155.

The Effects of Foods on Mood, Focus, and Performance

Now let's discuss some powerful, yet relatively unknown effects of the foods you eat. First, you need to understand that not all carbohydrate-based foods—the foods that form the base of the pyramid—are created equal. Sure, they all contain four calories per one-gram serving, but the speed at which they are converted into blood glucose varies greatly. This is important because large changes in blood glucose affect your energy level, mood, and focus. Furthermore, depending on your genetically set sensitivity to insulin (a hormone released to modulate blood sugar), the glucose can be converted to fat instead of utilized for immediate energy needs. This helps explain why some low-fat or no-fat "diet foods" such as SnackWell's cookies can be as fattening as regular cookies. Foods with high content of sugar or bleached flour (are they listed atop the ingredients label?) should be avoided as much as those with high saturated or trans-fat content.

Sound confusing? Fortunately, there's the Glycemic Index (GI), which distinguishes the good carbohydrate-based foods from those that are not so good. Foods with a high Glycemic Index cause a rapid increase in blood sugar, which results in a large insulin response. Low-GI foods produce more subtle variations and, hence, more stable energy levels, mood, and concentration. Consequently, the wise golfer eats mainly low- to medium-GI foods before and during play, and avoids high-index foods that are destined to throw off mental and physical performance. Ever find yourself on the back nine yawning, nodding off, or struggling to focus? There's a good chance it's the result of foods you've consumed before teeing off or at the turn.

Estimating the GI of foods is often more difficult than you might think. For instance, most foods classified as simple carbohydrates (cereal, sugar candies, some fruit juices) have a high GI. Yet so do potatoes, white rice, white bread, and bagels—all considered complex carbohydrates. Some low-GI foods are whole grains, brown rice, milk, and most fruits and vegetables. As a rule, the more processed and easily digestible a food, the higher its GI (for example, liquids have a higher GI than similar solids). High-fiber foods tend to elicit a slower insulin response and, thus, they have a lower GI.

Finally, foods containing some protein and fat along with the carbohydrate also come in lower on the scale. This bit of information is useful if you don't have the gumption to memorize and use this index. Consuming a small amount of protein and fat during each of your carbohydrate feedings serves to moderate the overall glycemic response to the meal. Again, try to form your meals and snacks so they fit the 60/20/20 macronutrient profile.

What About the Atkins and Zone Diets?

Diet fads are constantly changing and resurfacing through the media, but in recent years the Atkins and Zone diets have received the most publicity. As a health- and fitness-conscious golf pro, I am frequently asked about these diet strategies. While I do not wish to delve too deeply into this subject, I do have some strong beliefs I'll touch on here.

Both of these diets can produce significant weight loss given you follow the plan precisely and shun most, if not all, high-carbohydrate foods. Unfortunately, such a diet is difficult to maintain in the long term, and carbohydrate restriction is one of the last things serious athletes—golfers included—would want to engage in, since carbohydrate is the preferred fuel in the muscles.

The bottom line: If you are clinically obese, I suggest you engage in a doctor-prescribed diet and fitness program. If you are just ten or twenty pounds overweight, however, I suggest you follow the nutritional and fitness training advice in this chapter. By introducing just a few hours of exercise per week and by adopting the nutritional surveillance strategies described on page 154, you should lose about one pound per week. Make these exercise and nutritional habits permanent and you'll never need to go on a diet again!

Nutritional Tips for Peak Performance on the Links

As you now know, the things you eat and drink before and during a round can significantly impact performance. In fact, for advanced players the food and drink consumed along the way can give or take away the edge needed to play a personal-best round or win a tournament. A properly fueled and hydrated body maintains coordination, concentration, and energy levels better, especially in the hot and stressful situations common to golf. Conversely, consuming the wrong foods and beverages, or eating nothing at all, is a form of self-sabotage. You might as well add a few strokes to your handicap as a result.

As always, forget about what everyone else is eating in the clubhouse or on the course. Use your knowledge of relationship between nutrition and performance to elevate your play. Here are my top five performance-nutrition tips guaranteed to enhance your play.

1. **Avoid large amounts of food (a meal) in the two hours leading up to tee time.** Food in your digestive system diverts blood away from your brain and muscles, hampering concentration and physical performance. A meal two to three hours before play is ideal. Also, consume at least a quart of water during the three hours before play.

2. **Drink a pint of water each hour on the course (more in hot weather).** This means you'll need to pack two quart-sized water bottles (or refill a single bottle after the ninth hole) for the typical four-hour round. Remind yourself that dehydration degrades coordination and athletic performance, and drink up!

3. **Avoid caffeinated and alcoholic beverages.** While both have their place, neither belongs on the golf course. Here's why. As we all know, caffeine is a central nervous system stimulant. That's useful in sports requiring

intense lifting or running, but for complex motor skill sports such as golf it's a performance killer. Any more than a single cup of coffee or tea in the few hours before you play will contribute to jitters and interfere with your finely tuned swing.

Alcohol, of course, really kills your motor control, as well as your perception and judgment. Some people argue that alcohol reduces their awareness of pressure and muscular tension on the course. I respond that serious golfers learn to control pressure and tension with their minds (see chapter 6), and without giving up the fine-motor control needed to execute the strokes. Finally, both caffeine and alcohol are diuretics, which flies in the face of my advice in tip 2!

4. **Eat two snacks as you play: one around the fifth hole and the other after the ninth.** The ideal snack is a slow-release energy bar such as a Balance Bar (avoid any energy bar with high-fructose corn syrup first on the ingredients list), a piece of fruit, or some other mid– to low–Glycemic Index food or combination of foods. This ensures a steady release of carbohydrate into your bloodstream for stable energy levels throughout the round. Timing the snacks right is just as important since there is a lag time for actually getting the food broken down and into the bloodstream. Food eaten during the front nine kicks in while you're playing the back. Snacking on the back nine has less benefit unless you're planning to play a second round. Either way, keep drinking water throughout, since there's little lag time for absorption of water.

5. **Leave the halfway snack-house food for the caddy.** As I point out in tip 1, significant food just before or during play will hinder your performance. You're better off being a little hungry on the back nine than bonking on the fifteenth hole because of the burger, fries, pizza, or cheese nachos you ate at the snack house. The snacks prescribed in tip 4 will keep you going like the Energizer Bunny and, just maybe, hitting like a Tiger!

References and Resources

Brand-Miller, Jennie, et al. (2003) *The New Glucose Revolution: The Authoritative Guide to the Glycemic Index.* New York: Marlowe & Company.

Hörst, Eric J. (2003) *Mental Wings: A Seven-Step Life-Elevating Program for Uncommon Success.* www.MentalWings.com.

Orlick, Terry. (2000) *In Pursuit of Excellence.* Champaign, IL: Human Kinetics.

Schmidt, Richard B., and Craig A. Wrisberg. (1991) *Motor Learning and Performance: From Principles to Practice.* Champaign, IL: Human Kinetics.

Ungerleider, Steven. (1996) *Mental Training for Peak Performance.* Emmaus, PA: Rodale Press.

Web Resources

Lisa Ann Hörst . . . . www.LisaAnnHorst.com
Ladies Professional Golf Association . . . . www.LPGA.com
Professional Golf Association . . . . www.PGA.com
Find-A-Lesson . . . . www.FindALesson.com
Golf Training Aids . . . . www.PracticeRange.com
Mental Game Mastery . . . . www.MentalGameMastery.com
Women's Golf ProShop. . . . . www.WomensGolfProshop.com
Electronic Putting Challenge . . . . www.GL-Tech.com
Golf Magazine Online . . . . www.GolfOnLine.com
Golf Digest Online . . . . www.GolfDigest.com
Golf Tips Online . . . . www.GolfTipsMag.com
Golf For Women Online . . . . www.GolfDigest.com/gfw

Afterword

It is often pointed out that golf is a great metaphor for life, and I agree completely. In fact, I believe that pursuing excellence in golf is fundamentally the same process as for improving performance and achieving excellence in any life area. All human performance evolves from the inside out—the quality of our thoughts and the actions that follow are almost entirely the determining factors as to how successful we become in any endeavor. Therefore, it is my hope that *Golf Training* will inspire you to act more thoughtfully and purposefully, whether it's at the driving range, on the golf course, at work, or around home.

As a final thought, I'd like you to ponder how this wonderful sport has enriched your life—consider the rush of a perfectly struck tee shot, the exhilaration of playing a personal-best round, and the glorious feeling of just walking the links on a perfect day. We are blessed to be able to challenge ourselves and recreate in this way, while so many people around the world are struggling just to survive. Given this perspective, I encourage you to live each day with an attitude of gratitude and to contribute some of your "golf power" to the world. There is no better exercise than reaching down and lifting up others. Look for ways to brighten the days of everyone you meet, and consider contributing some time or money to aid those who are less fortunate. I invite you to check out a few of my favorite charities, listed below.

www.WorldVision.org
www.MakeAWish.org
www.TheFirstTee.org

About the Author

After beating a life-threatening illness as a young child, Lisa Ann Hörst began golfing at age seven with her father, mother, and three brothers. Quickly excelling in the sport, she began competing at age ten. Not being one to pass up on any challenge, she tried out for—and made—the boys' high school golf team, which she co-captained her senior year. Lisa Ann won numerous amateur tournaments and was named to the PING All-American Juniors Team. She went on to attend Penn State University on a golf scholarship, where she earned a degree in kinesiology—a course of study that helped give birth to her golf training philosophy.

After graduation, Lisa Ann joined the LPGA teaching division and has achieved the rank of Class A teaching professional. An LPGA pro for more than fifteen years, she currently teaches at Leisure Lanes Golf Center and Groff's Farm Golf Club. In addition to her teaching career, Lisa Ann has found time to write and speak on the subjects of training and motivation, do charity work, dabble in sports modeling, and even become an accomplished rock climber. Her instructional articles and tips have appeared in *Golf Digest, Golf Tips, Golf Illustrated,* and other magazines, and on the national One-On-One Sports Radio network (now The Sporting News Radio network).

Lisa Ann lives in Lancaster, Pennsylvania, with her husband, Eric, and two sons, Cameron and Jonathan. Learn more about Lisa Ann and her golf training techniques at *www.LisaAnnHorst.com.*

L.A. Hörst with her sons, Jonathan and Cameron, and her husband, Eric.